ARABIC POET
FOR STUDENTS

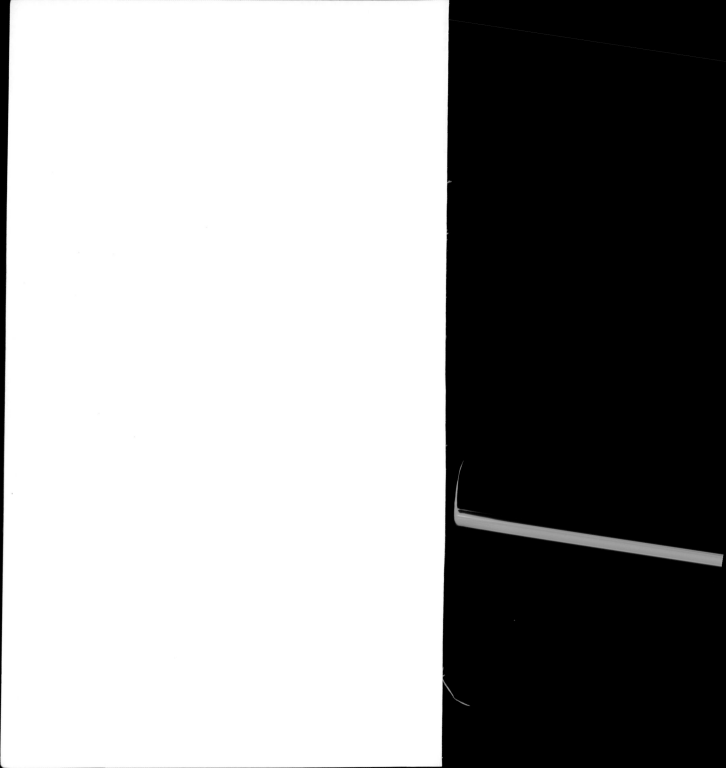

ARABIC POETRY

A PRIMER FOR STUDENTS

BY

A. J. ARBERRY

LITT.D., F.B.A.

Sir Thomas Adams's Professor of Arabic
in the University of Cambridge

CAMBRIDGE

AT THE UNIVERSITY PRESS

1965

CAMBRIDGE UNIVERSITY PRESS
Cambridge, New York, Melbourne, Madrid, Cape Town, Singapore,
São Paulo, Delhi, Dubai, Tokyo, Mexico City

Cambridge University Press
The Edinburgh Building, Cambridge CB2 8RU, UK

Published in the United States of America by
Cambridge University Press, New York

www.cambridge.org
Information on this title: www.cambridge.org/9780521092579

First published 1965
Re-issued 2010

A catalogue record for this publication is available from the British Library

Library of Congress Catalogue Card Number: 65-11206

ISBN 978-0-521-04037-2 Hardback
ISBN 978-0-521-09257-9 Paperback

CONTENTS

AUTHOR'S NOTE

I am grateful to my friend and colleague Professor R. B. Serjeant who read the proofs and made a number of valuable suggestions. Proposals for amended text or interpretation from other scholars will be warmly welcomed.

Students may find it convenient to read the following poems before the rest: 4, 5, 8, 19, 25, 2, 1, 3.

INTRODUCTION

"The most striking feature in Arabic literature is its unexpectedness. Over and over again, with scarcely a hint to give warning of what is coming, a new literary art emerges fully-fledged, often with a perfection never equalled by later exponents of the same art. Nowhere is this element of surprise more striking than in the first appearance of Arabic as a vehicle of literature. At one moment Arabia seems, in a literary sense, empty and dumb except for some votive or businesslike inscriptions in a variety of dialects. At the next, companies of poets spring up all over northern Arabia, reciting complex odes, *qaṣīdas*, in which a series of themes are elaborated with unsurpassed vigour, vividness of imagination, and precision of imagery, in an infinitely rich and highly articulated language, showing little or no traces of dialect, and cast into complex and flexible metrical schemes that rhyme throughout the poem."[1]

"It is impossible to fix with any degree of certainty the date when the Arabs first began to practise the art of poetry. The oldest poets of whom we have any remains belong to the time of the War of al-Basûs, or shortly before that, which would place them about a hundred and thirty years before the Flight [A.D. 622]. But these are spoken of, not as the inventors of the poetic art, but as the authorities for the laws of the *Ḳaṣîdah* or ode, a form of composition which is subject to very rigid conventions as to the contents and sequence of its parts. What we possess of the distinguished poets to whom these laws were due is cast in forms which we cannot but suppose to be the outcome of a long education in the construction of verse. The number and complexity of the measures which they use, their established laws of quantity and rhyme, and the uniform manner in which they introduce the subjects of their poems, notwithstanding the distance which often separated one composer from another, all point to a long previous study and cultivation of the art of expression and the capacities of their language, a study of which no record now remains. In the earliest poems, as they now stand, when we compare them with those of fifty or a hundred years later, we can detect little that is archaic or immature. Indeed, one of the most ancient of the group, Imra-al-Ḳais, is generally esteemed the greatest of them, and was so judged of by Muḥammad himself.

[1] Sir Hamilton Gibb, *Arabic Literature* (2nd edition, Clarendon Press, 1963), p. 13.

"After this first outburst of song the cultivation of the art extended with immense rapidity. Except the distant 'Omân and Mahrah, where the Ḥimyaritic or an allied speech still survived, no part of Arabia was without its poets. The 'Language of Ma'add'—that is, the speech of the Central and so-called Ishmaelite Arabs,—had by this time taken possession of the whole of al-Yaman except the coasts of the Indian Ocean; the supremacy of the *Tubba's* or Ḥimyarite Kings over the rest of the Peninsula had passed away for ever; and in the course of the sixth century after Christ the last traces of it were obliterated when the Kings of Kindah were driven, with their people, from al-Yamâmah and Hajar back to their original inheritance in Ḥaḍramaut. A great uniformity of speech overspread the land, whether due, as is usually assumed, to the general observance of the Pilgrimage to Mekkah and the meeting of the tribes at 'Ukâḍh, or to some other cause. The same masculine and expressive language was heard from al-Ḥîrah on the Euphrates, under the shadow of Persia, and Ghassân in Syria, beneath the great cathedral of Damascus, to Ṣan'â and Aden in the far South, where a Persian governor ruled in the name of the Shâhanshâh, and the profession of the poet was everywhere honoured and rewarded. 'When there appeared a poet in a family of the Arabs, the other tribes round about would gather together to that family and wish them joy of their good luck. Feasts would be got ready, the women of the tribe would join together in bands, playing upon lutes, as they were wont to do at bridals, and the men and boys would congratulate one another; for a poet was a defence to the honour of them all, a weapon to ward off insult from their good name, and a means of perpetuating their glorious deeds and of establishing their fame for ever. And they used not to wish one another joy but for three things—the birth of a boy, the coming to light of a poet, and the foaling of a noble mare.'"[1]

"By the ancient Arabs the poet (*shá'ir*, plural *shu'ará*), as his name implies, was held to be a person endowed with supernatural knowledge, a wizard in league with spirits (*jinn*) or satans (*shayáṭín*) and dependent on them for the magical powers which he displayed. This view of his personality, as well as the influential position which he occupied, are curiously indicated by the story of a certain youth who was refused the hand of his beloved on the ground that he was neither a poet nor a soothsayer nor a water-diviner. The idea of poetry as an

[1] Sir Charles Lyall, *Translations of Ancient Arabian Poetry* (Williams and Norgate, 1930), pp. xv–xvii. The citation is from Ibn Rashīq (d. 456/1064) as quoted by al-Suyūṭī, *al-Muzhir*, II, 236.

art was developed afterwards; the pagan *shá'ir* is the oracle of his tribe, their guide in peace and their champion in war....

"Besides fountain-songs, war-songs, and hymns to idols, other kinds of poetry must have existed in the earliest times—*e.g.*, the love-song and the dirge. The powers of the *shá'ir*, however, were chiefly exhibited in Satire (*hijá*)....The menaces which he hurled against the foe were believed to be inevitably fatal. His rhymes, often compared to arrows, had all the effect of a solemn curse spoken by a divinely inspired prophet or priest, and their pronunciation was attended with peculiar ceremonies of a symbolic character, such as anointing the hair on one side of the head, letting the mantle hang down loosely, and wearing only one sandal. Satire retained something of these ominous associations at a much later period when the magic utterance of the *shá'ir* had long given place to the lampoon by which the poet reviles his enemies and holds them up to shame.

"The obscure beginnings of Arabian poetry, presided over by the magician and his familiar spirits, have left not a rack behind in the shape of literature, but the task of reconstruction is comparatively easy where we are dealing with a people so conservative and tenacious of antiquity as the Arabs. Thus it may be taken for certain that the oldest form of poetical speech in Arabia was rhyme without metre (*Saj'*), or, as we should say, 'rhymed prose,' although the fact of Muḥammad's adversaries calling him a poet because he used it in the Koran shows the light in which it was regarded even after the invention and elaboration of metre. Later on, as we shall see, *Saj'* became a merely rhetorical ornament, the distinguishing mark of all eloquence whether spoken or written, but originally it had a deeper, almost religious, significance as the special form adopted by poets, soothsayers, and the like in their supernatural revelations and for conveying to the vulgar every kind of mysterious and esoteric lore."[1]

The foregoing quotations from three eminent authorities sum up all that is known, and much that has been speculated, concerning the origins and earliest history of Arabic poetry. It is most unlikely that more than this will ever be known, saving some miraculous discovery in the unexplored caves of Arabia of an Arabic counterpart of the Dead Sea Scrolls; and even such a remote contingency recedes still farther into the improbable when

[1] R. A. Nicholson, *A Literary History of the Arabs* (T. Fisher Unwin, 1907), pp. 72–4.

it is remembered that the art of writing was little practised amongst the ancient Arabs, and that for long decades poetry was transmitted not by careful script but from mouth to mouth.[1] The abundant remains of that desert literature, saved for posterity by the enthusiastic labours of the Arab Humanists,[2] confront us with a truly astonishing phenomenon, the marvel of which familiarity can never wholly dim. There in the sandy wastes, upon the very fringes of settled civilisation, a group of scattered and perennially warring tribes united only in the possession of a common language invented, and brought to a high state of refinement without benefit of schoolmen, a form of poetry unique in its kind, of complex prosody and dazzling imagery.

The fashion which they set maintained itself virtually unaltered down to the end of the Umayyad period (A.D. 750), and though challenged by some daring spirits under the 'Abbásid Caliphate, speedily reasserted its supremacy, which at the present day is almost as absolute as ever.[3]

The relics of ancient Arabic poetry fall into two categories: the *qaṣīda* or ode (the fashion referred to in the immediately preceding quotation), and the *qiṭ'a* or "occasional" piece. Concerning the latter group, well represented in famous anthologies (such for instance as the *Kitāb al-Ḥamāsa* of Abū Tammām, an eminent poet in his own right who died in A.D. 846), two theories have been advanced: one, that they are fragments remembered out of lost longer poems, the other that they are originally independent poems composed on individual themes and in particular contexts.

It has been customary to think of poems dealing with individual themes as *ḳiṭ'ahs*, or parts of the *ḳaṣīdah*, as if perhaps they were derived from it. It seems to me more reasonable to consider the *ḳaṣīdah* as built up of a number of *ḳiṭ'ahs*. Let us recall that most of the ancient *ḳaṣīdahs* were sung, and the poet while still not warmed to his work is casting about amongst the conventionalised phrasery and themes so well known to him and his listeners that a verse can almost automatically

[1] The theory that all, or most, pre-Islamic poetry is a forgery has now been generally abandoned.

[2] For their names and dates see Lyall, *op. cit.* pp. xxxix–xl.

[3] Nicholson, *op. cit.* p. 76.

be produced from them. Once warmed to his task the true subject of the poem is declaimed with vigour and point. Now, I do not mean that the classical *ḳaṣīdah* of Muhammad's time was invariably produced in this way, for it seems that poets then composed by reflection, set pieces, as one would expect in a highly civilised community, and by no means relied on extempore performance alone. But the *ḳaṣīdah* form was based fundamentally on a form which arose from conditions under which poetry was composed extempore.[1]

Whatever the truth may be, there is no disputing the fact that the full-length and fully articulated *qaṣīda* was esteemed as the only valid form of "classical" poetry. The pattern of the ode had rapidly become highly conventionalised, and is as described in a famous passage from the writings of an early critic.[2]

I have heard from a man of learning that the composer of Odes began by mentioning the deserted dwelling-places and the relics and traces of habitation. Then he wept and complained and addressed the desolate encampment, and begged his companion to make a halt, in order that he might have occasion to speak of those who had once lived there and afterwards departed; for the dwellers in tents were different from townsmen or villagers in respect of coming and going, because they moved from one water-spring to another, seeking pasture and searching out the places where rain had fallen. Then to this he linked the erotic prelude (*nasíb*), and bewailed the violence of his love and the anguish of separation from his mistress and the extremity of his passion and desire, so as to win the hearts of his hearers and divert their eyes towards him and invite their ears to listen to him, since the song of love touches men's souls and takes hold of their hearts, God having put it in the constitution of His creatures to love dalliance and the society of women, in such wise that we find very few but are attached thereto by some tie or have some share therein, whether lawful or unpermitted. Now, when the poet had assured himself of an attentive hearing, he followed up his advantage and set forth his claim: thus he went on to complain of fatigue and want of sleep and travelling by night and of the noonday heat, and how his camel had been reduced to leanness. And when, after representing all the discomfort and danger of his journey, he knew that he had fully justified his hope and

[1] R. B. Serjeant, *Prose and Poetry from Ḥaḍramawt* (Taylor's Foreign Press, 1951), pp. 56–7.

[2] Ibn Qutaiba, *Kitāb al-Shi'r wa'l-Shu'arā'*, pp. 14–15. The translation is by R. A. Nicholson.

expectation of receiving his due meed from the person to whom the poem was addressed, he entered upon the panegyric (*madīḥ*), and incited him to reward, and kindled his generosity by exalting him above his peers and pronouncing the greatest dignity, in comparison with his, to be little.

Many thousands of poems have been composed, even down to modern times, in close conformity with the pattern as set out in the foregoing lines; so much so, that contemporary descriptions of "the discomfort and danger of his journey" have elaborated the theme afresh, only substituting for the traditional camel more up-to-date means of locomotion—the railway train, the motor-car, even the aeroplane. Out of the great mass of ancient desert *qaṣīdas*—"the general similarity in structure and content of the pre-Islamic odes may give, especially when they are read in translation, an impression of monotony, almost of bareness, mirroring with a certain rude force the uniformity of desert life, its concreteness, realism, absence of shading and of introspection"[1]—supremacy in excellence has from very early times been awarded to a small group of poems by different authors, known as *al-Mu'allaqāt* ("The Suspended Ones"). I have recently given a full account, and new translations, of these poems in *The Seven Odes*, to which the attention of the reader is invited for further information about this group in particular and the ancient poetry in general.

To this restriction of permitted themes were added other conventions no less hampering in their own way to the free play of the poetic imagination. The ode was, and is, required to open with a rhyming couplet—the couplet, called *bait*, being regarded as a unit of composition, is made up of two hemistichs or *miṣrā'*—and the rhyme so enunciated is maintained throughout the ensuing poem, which may range in length from above twenty to a hundred or so couplets. (With rare exceptions, only the opening couplet is doubly rhymed.) The rhymes are usually feminine; thus, in the poem of al-Samau'al included in this selection, we find jam*īlu*, sab*īlu*, qal*īlu*, etc.; in the poem of 'Antara, il-lay*ālī*, shim*ālī*, bi-*bālī*,

[1] Gibb, *op. cit.* p. 21.

etc. Even allowing for the extraordinary richness in rhyme of the Arabic language, the necessity of building so many identical rhymes into a poetic sequence, and of contriving that their successive occurrence should appear perfectly natural and indeed inevitable, called for virtuosity of the very first order. Since it was moreover considered a blemish to allow the structure of a sentence to run over from one couplet to the next, so that each couplet was thought of as a complete rhetorical statement, the greatest ingenuity was needed to concatenate the several statements together to create the impression of a continuous, or at any rate harmonious narration.

As if to compensate for these and the like restrictions, the poet was presented with a remarkably wide choice of rhythmical patterns, or metres, in which to express his thoughts; though once the choice was made, the same metre had to be sustained throughout the individual poem. Though the poets from earliest times employed this range of complicated rhythms with almost unvarying accuracy, their structures were first successfully analysed during the eighth century by the grammarian al-Khalīl ibn Aḥmad of Basra (died *ca.* A.D. 790).

> Both al-Ḥarīrī and Ibn Khallikān report that al-Khalīl had noticed the different rhythms produced by the hammering in different copper-workshops in the bazaar in Basra, and that this gave him the idea of developing a science of metre, in other words, of determining the rhythm in the structure of the ancient poems.[1]

The system and nomenclature invented by al-Khalīl have formed the accepted basis of all subsequent investigation.

It has been generally agreed, alike by ancient and modern scholars, that the earliest metre to be invented by the Arabs is that known as *rajaz*, "a measure said to correspond with the lifting and lowering of the camel's feet".[2] In the old poetry this metre was distinguished from all others by the fact that *every* hemistich

[1] G. Weil in *Encyclopaedia of Islam*², I, p. 669. The student is recommended to study this whole masterly exposition of *'Arūḍ*.

[2] H. G. Farmer, *A History of Arabian Music* (Luzac and Co., 1929), p. 14. This work contains valuable information on the part played by singing and instrumental music in the chanting of Arabic poetry. For a different interpretation of the basic meaning of *rajaz*, see Nicholson, *op. cit.* p. 74.

rhymed; "the more modern, on the contrary, not infrequently follow the rule of the other metres in rhyming only the second hemistich of each verse".[1] The following scheme indicates the rhythmic variations allowed in the use of this ancient, flexible and, by the most part of professional poets, despised metre.[2]

Trimeter acatalectic	⏒ – ⏑ – | ⏒ – ⏑ – | ⏒ – ⏑ –
	⏓ ⏑ ⏑ – | ⏓ ⏑ ⏑ – | ⏓ ⏑ ⏑ –
Trimeter catalectic	⏒ – ⏑ – | ⏒ – ⏑ – | ⏒ – –
	⏓ ⏑ ⏑ – | ⏓ ⏑ ⏑ – | ⏒ – –
Dimeter acatalectic	⏒ – ⏑ – | ⏒ – ⏑ –
	⏓ ⏑ ⏑ – | ⏓ ⏑ ⏑ –
Dimeter catalectic	⏒ – ⏑ – | ⏒ – –
	⏓ ⏑ ⏑ – | ⏒ – –

In this selection, the poem by Ibn al-Mu'tazz illustrates the antique convention of all hemistichs rhyming together, within the trimeter catalectic variation.

– – ⏑ – | – – ⏑ – | ⏑ – –
lammā tafarrā l-ufqu bi-l-ḍiyā'i

– – ⏑ – | – ⏑ ⏑ – | – – –
mithla btisāmi l-shafati l-lamyā'i

The poem by Maṭrān, in trimeter acatalectic, follows the regular *qaṣīda* rhyming scheme.

– ⏑ ⏑ – | – ⏑ ⏑ – | ⏑ – ⏑ –
shāda fa-a'lā wa-banā fa-waṭṭadā

– – ⏑ – | ⏑ – ⏑ – | – – ⏑ –
lā lil-'ulā wa-lā lahū bal lil-'idā

The ode by Mihyār al-Dailamī employs the same metre and rhyming scheme.

The *ṭawīl*, "one of the finest, as well as the most common, of the Arabic metres"[3] extensively employed in heroic and panegyric verse, is represented in this collection by the poems of al-Samau'al, al-Nābigha, al-Mutanabbī, Abū Firās, Ibn 'Unain, Ibn al-Fāriḍ

[1] W. Wright, *A Grammar of the Arabic Language* (3rd edition, Cambridge, 1951), II, 362.

[2] "Between these highly developed productions and the rude doggerel of *Saj'* or *Rajaz* there lies an interval, the length of which it is impossible even to conjecture" (Nicholson, *op. cit.* p. 75). In the Muslim Middle Ages the *rajaz* was extensively employed in mnemonic manuals on grammar, medicine, mathematics, etc. Note that Arabic metrics are quantitative.

[3] Wright, *op. cit.* II, p. 264.

and al-Bārūdī. (Robert Browning in his *Abt Vogler* gave a passable English imitation.)[1] The following is the pattern of its regular acatalectic variety.

⏑ – ⏒ | ⏑ – ⏓ – | ⏑ – ⏒ | ⏑ – ⏑ – || ⏑ – ⏒ | ⏑ – ⏓ – | ⏑ – ⏒ | ⏑ – ⏑ –

⏑ – – | ⏑ – – – | ⏑ – ⏑ | ⏑ – ⏑ –
atānī abaita l-la'na annaka lumtanī

⏑ – – | ⏑ – – – | ⏑ – – | ⏑ – ⏑ –
wa-tilka llatī ahtammu minhā wa-anṣabu (al-Nābigha)

In this variety, the last foot sometimes occurs in a different form.

⏑ – – | ⏑ – – – | ⏑ – ⏑ | ⏑ – ⏑ –
sharibnā 'alā dhikri l'ḥabībi mudāmatan

⏑ – – | ⏑ – – – | ⏑ – – | ⏑ – – –
sakirnā bihā min qablu an yukhlaqa l-karmú (Ibn al-Fāriḍ)

The catalectic variety is as follows.

⏑ – ⏒ | ⏑ – ⏓ – | ⏑ – ⏒ | ⏑ – ⏑ – || ⏑ – ⏒ | ⏑ – ⏓ – | ⏑ – ⏑ | ⏑ – –

⏑ – – | ⏑ – – – | ⏑ – – | ⏑ – ⏑ –
idhā l-mar'u lam yadnas mina l-lu'mi 'irḍuhú

⏑ – ⏑ | ⏑ – – – | ⏑ – ⏑ | ⏑ – –
fa-kullu ridā'in yartadīhi jamīlú (al-Samau'al)

Another extremely popular metre is the *basīṭ*, here represented by al-Khansā', Abū Tammām, Ibn Zaidūn and al-Shidyāq. The tetrameter is the commonest form, and has this pattern.

⏒ – ⏑ – | ⏓ ⏑ – | ⏒ – ⏑ – | ⏑ ⏑ – || ⏒ – ⏑ – | ⏓ ⏑ – | ⏒ – ⏑ – | ⏕ –

– – ⏑ – | ⏑ ⏑ – | – – ⏑ – | ⏑ ⏑ –
innī ariqtu fa-bittu l-laila sāhiratan

⏑ – | ⏑ – | ⏑ ⏑ – | – – ⏑ – | – –
ka-annamā kuḥilat 'ainī bi-'uwwārí (al-Khansā')

A third heroic metre is the *kāmil*, found in trimeter (acatalectic and catalectic) and dimeter. The following is the pattern of the acatalectic trimeter.

⏕ – ⏑ – | ⏕ – ⏑ – | ⏕ – ⏑ – || ⏕ – ⏑ – | ⏕ – ⏑ – | ⏕ – ⏑ –

– – ⏑ – | ⏑ ⏑ – ⏑ – | – – ⏑ –
al-arḍu qad labisat ridā'an akhḍarā

– – ⏑ – | ⏑ ⏑ – ⏑ – | – – ⏑ –
wa-l-ṭallu yanthuru fī rubāhā jauharā (Ibn Sahl)

[1] See Lyall, *op. cit.* p. xlix.

The catalectic variety runs thus.

⏑⏑ – ⏑ – | ⏑⏑ – ⏑ – | ⏑⏑ – ⏑ – || ⏑⏑ – ⏑ – | ⏑⏑ – ⏑ – | ⏑⏑ – –

– – ⏑ – | ⏑ ⏑ – ⏑ – | ⏑ ⏑ – ⏑ –
ṣafwun utīḥa fa-khudh li-nafsika qisṭahā

– – ⏑ – | ⏑ ⏑ – ⏑ – | ⏑ ⏑ – –
fa-l-ṣafwu laisa ʿalā l-madā bi-mutāḥi (Shauqī)

The dimeter *kāmil* as here illustrated is of the form called *muraffal* ("having a train"), so-named because a syllable is added to lengthen the second half of the verse. In the dimeter form, the last word of the first half of the verse is frequently divided, its concluding part being the opening of the second half.

⏑⏑ – ⏑ – | ⏑⏑ – ⏑ – || ⏑⏑ – ⏑ – | ⏑⏑ – ⏑ – | –

– – ⏑ – | ⏑ ⏑ – ⏑ –
idh naḥnu fī ghurafi l-jinā—

⏑ ⏑ – ⏑ – | – – ⏑ – | –
ni naʿūmu fī baḥri l-surūri (Abu 'l-ʿAtāhiya)

The *wāfir* is substantially a reversed version of the *kāmil*.

⏑ – ⏑⏑ – | ⏑ – ⏑⏑ – | ⏑ – – || ⏑ – ⏑⏑ – | ⏑ – ⏑⏑ – | ⏑ – –

⏑ – – – | ⏑ – ⏑⏑ – | ⏑ – –
nufūsun lil-qiyāmati tashraʾibbu

⏑ – – – | ⏑ – ⏑⏑ – | ⏑ – –
wa-ghaiyun fī l-baṭālati mutlaʾibbu (al-Maʿarrī)

A very common metre is the *khafīf*, which is encountered in both dimeter and trimeter, acatalectic and catalectic. In this selection it is illustrated in poems by ʿAntara, Bashshār, Ibn al-Rūmī, al-Buḥturī, Ibn Zuhr (in a *muwashshaḥa*, of which more hereafter) and al-Ruṣāfī. Here is the trimeter acatalectic.

⏓ ⏑ – – | ⏓ – ⏑ – | ⏓ ⏑ – – || ⏓ ⏑ – – | ⏓ – ⏑ – | ⏓ ⏑ – –

– ⏑ – – | – – ⏑ – | – ⏑ – –
ḥāribīnī yā nāʾibāti l-layālī

– ⏑ – – | ⏑ – ⏑ – | – ⏑ – –
ʿan yamīnī wa-tāratan ʿan shimālī (ʿAntara)

And here is the dimeter acatalectic.

⏓ ⏑ – – | ⏓ – ⏑ – || ⏓ ⏑ – – | ⏓ – ⏑ –

– ⏑ – – | – – ⏑ –
ṭāla lailī min ḥubbi man

– ⏑ – – | ⏑ – ⏑ –
lā urābū muqāribī (Bashshār)

The *ramal*, here shown in poems by ʻUmar ibn Abī Rabīʻa and Ibn Zākūr (the latter a *muwashshaḥa*), also occurs in dimeter and trimeter with the same variations. The specimen given is of the trimeter acatalectic.

⏒ ⏑ – – | ⏒ ⏑ – – | ⏒ ⏑ – ‖ ⏒ ⏑ – – | ⏒ ⏑ – – | ⏒ ⏑ –

– ⏑ – – | – ⏑ – – | – ⏑ –
laita Hindan anjazatnā mā taʻid

⏑ ⏑ – – | ⏑ ⏑ – – | – ⏑ –
wa-shafat anfusanā mimmā tajid

(ʻUmar ibn Abī Rabīʻa)

The *mutaqārib* is a tripping measure more commonly used in Persian (it is the metre of the *Shāh-nāma* and many other epics) than in Arabic. The example offered is of the acatalectic variety.

⏑ – ⏒ | ⏑ – ⏒ | ⏑ – ⏒ | ⏑ – ‖ ⏑ – ⏒ | ⏑ – ⏒ | ⏑ – ⏒ | ⏑ – –

⏑ – – | ⏑ – – | ⏑ – – | ⏑ –
saqānī bi-ʻainaihi shibha llatī

⏑ – – | ⏑ – – | ⏑ – – | ⏑ – –
bi-kaffaihi hādhā l-aghannu l-rashīqú (Ibn al-Khaiyāṭ)

The *sarīʻ* is a fairly variable metre.

⏒ ⏓ ⏑ – | ⏒ ⏓ ⏑ – | – ⏑ – ‖ ⏒ ⏓ ⏑ – | ⏒ ⏓ ⏑ – | – –

⏑ – ⏑ – | – – ⏑ – | – ⏑ –
wa-ḍaifi ṭaifin amma min hājirin

– ⏑ ⏑ – | – – ⏑ – | – –
bāta bihi l-mashkuwwu mashkūrā (Ibn Khafāja)

The *mujtathth* is fairly rare in Arabic, somewhat commoner in Persian poetry. The concluding word of the first half of the verse often runs over into the second half.

⏒ – ⏑ – | ⏒ ⏑ – – ‖ ⏒ – ⏑ – | ⏖ – –

– – ⏑ – | ⏑ ⏑ – –
yā dīna qalbika min bā—

⏑ – ⏑ – | ⏑ ⏑ – –
riqin yunīru wa-yakhbū (al-Sharīf al-Raḍī)

The *madīd* is a rare metre, usually catalectic.

⏒ ⏑ – – | ⏒ ⏑ – | ⏒ ⏑ – ‖ ⏒ ⏑ – – | ⏒ ⏑ – | ⏖ –

– ⏑ – – | – ⏑ – | ⏑ ⏑ –
lā takhaf ithman wa-lā ḥarajan

⏑ ⏑ – | – – ⏑ – | – –
fa-damu l-ʻushshāqi maṭlūlú (Bahā' al-Dīn Zuhair)

Another rare metre is the *muqtaḍab*: it may be scanned in either two or three feet, the first alternative here being preferred.

⏓ ∪ – | ∪ – | ∪ ∪ – || ⏒ ∪ – | ∪ – | ∪ ∪ –

– ∪ – | ∪ – | ∪ ∪ –
ḥāmilu l-hawā taʿibú

– ∪ – | ∪ – | ∪ ∪ –
yastakhiffuhu l-ṭarabú (Abū Nuwās)

For the scansion of the other metres, and for a more detailed analysis, together with an account of the various licenses and the rules governing the rhyme, the student should consult Wright's *Arabic Grammar*, II, 350–90.

Such was, and is, the great variety of metres available to the Arab poet, so that it would be no exaggeration to say that rhythm is the most outstanding characteristic of the Arabian Muse. (Inasmuch as the subtle nuances of these variable rhythms are inimitable in any European language, it necessarily follows that all western translations of Arabic poetry, however artfully contrived, fail utterly to convey the immense range of moods expressed in his rhythmic incantations by the Arab poet.) It seems more likely, than any other theory that has been propounded, that the inspiration and precise execution of these poetical rhythms derived from the art of drumming, the most basic of all forms of music.

In the pre-Islamic period poets employed preponderantly the longer metres in their declaimed *qaṣīdas*, notably the *ṭawīl*, the *wāfir*, the *kāmil* and the *basīṭ*. This is not to say that the shorter metres were not also used, as might indeed by expected in a society which already enjoyed the seductive pleasures of lute, reed-pipe and singing-girl. But the martial virtues attracted the widest admiration in that land of perpetual feuds. With the spread and consolidation of the Islamic Empire, the lyric of love and wine came more and more into favour; princes had greater leisure than Bedouin chieftains to listen to soft music and to savour dancing and song. Hence, from the Umaiyad times of ʿUmar ibn Abī Rabīʿa onwards, and especially in the Abbasid palaces amused by the like of Abū Nuwās, whilst for serious occasions the long measures of the *qaṣīda* continued to enjoy pride of esteem, more and more songs, ancestors of the Persian *ghazal*, won for their cunning composers comparable rewards.

A change in vocabulary accompanied this change in measures. At once the glory and the baffling challenge of the ancient odes stemmed from the inexhaustible repertory of rare and numinous words at the command of the great poets. Natural endowment (*ṭab*ʿ) required the enhancement of art (*ṣanʿa*) to secure respect and recognition; it was not unusual for a poet to labour for months revising and refining a single ode.[1] It is thus not surprising that even in antiquity the learned commentators on the ancient poems were not seldom at a loss to understand the precise significance of a word or a phrase; for modern students the task of interpretation is always burdensome and sometimes intolerable. (For this reason, in the present anthology these fine but difficult poems have been omitted; the student will prefer to tackle them at a later stage; and in any case, reliable translations of a great part of the pre-Islamic poetry are readily available.) Whilst through all the succeeding centuries there has never been any lack of learned poets who loved to parade their erudition, and to give employment to exegetes, with the spread of Islam and the ever wider diffusion of the Arabic language amongst peoples who formerly used other tongues, many poets preferred a simpler diction to match the gentler cadences of the new music.

From the earliest times, the poets had vied with one another in the invention and elaboration of rhetorical figures. In the beginning these were largely confined to the metaphor and the simile, but these were marshalled and displayed in close abundance. So, Imra' al-Qais delights to dwell on the remembered charms of a former mistress.

I twisted her side-tresses to me, and she leaned over me;
slender-waisted she was, and tenderly plump her ankles,
shapely and taut her belly, white-fleshed, not the least flabby,
polished the lie of her breast-bones, smooth as a burnished mirror.
She turns away, to show a soft cheek, and wards me off
with the glance of a wild deer of Wajra, a shy gazelle with its fawn;

[1] Thus, Zuhair, author of one of the *Muʿallaqāt*, would think nothing of spending a year on a *qaṣīda*; see Shauqī Ḍaif, *al-Fann wa-madhāhibuh fī 'l-shiʿr al-ʿArabī*, p. 18.

she shows me a throat like the throat of an antelope, not ungainly
when she lifts it upwards, neither naked of ornament;
she shows me her thick black tresses, a dark embellishment
clustering down her back like bunches of a laden date-tree—
twisted upwards meanwhile are the locks that ring her brow,
the knots cunningly lost in the plaited and loosened strands;
she shows me a waist slender and slight as a camel's nose-rein,
and a smooth shank like the reed of a watered, bent papyrus.
In the morning the grains of musk hang over her couch,
sleeping the forenoon through, not girded and aproned to labour.
She gives with fingers delicate, not coarse; you might say
they are sand-worms of Zaby, or tooth-sticks of ishil-wood.
At eventide she lightens the black shadows, as if she were
the lamp kindled in the night of a monk at his devotions.

This immensely rich vocabulary of images, the mythology of the Jāhilī poets, was gratefully accepted by their heirs down the centuries, whose joyous care it was to enlarge the repertory and to invent ever new variations upon the well-worn and well-loved themes.

The poets [writes Ibn Ḥazm in his *Ṭauq al-ḥamāma*[1]] have wonderful skill in inventing metaphorical allusions. Allow me to quote a stanza or two of mine in this vein.

The clouds were shooting from on high
Their slender arrows through the sky;
Like drawn and molten silver thread
The rains were falling overhead.

A crescent moon in blackest night
Stooped from his firmament of light;
Proclaim the lover who attained!
The inconceivable he gained;

So inconceivable, that should
You ask, "What have you there?" I could
No words discover, and no wile
Devise for answer, but a smile.

A smile so joyous, it might seem
My happiness was but a dream,
My joy so overwhelming, too,
I doubted if it could be true.

[1] See my *The Ring of the Dove* (Luzac, 1953), pp. 247–8.

This is another poem I wrote in the same mood.

You came to me, that witching time
The crescent moon climbed up on high,
Ere yet the sweet and clamorous chime
Of Christian bells rang through the sky.

My crescent moon was like the brow
Of some grave scholar, white as snow,
The instep delicate, I trow,
Of lovely maid its graceful bow.

And suddenly God's rainbow drew
Its arc across the heavens pale,
Apparalled in each dazzling hue
That glitters from the peacock's tail.

Elsewhere in the same book we find the author ingenuously boasting of his rare skill in crowding ornament.[1]

I am the shepherd of the skies,
  Deputed to preserve
The planets as they sink and rise,
  The stars that do not swerve.

Those, as they swing their lamps above
  Our earth, by night possessed,
Are like the kindled fires of love
  Within my darkling breast.

Or I am now the gardener
  Of some green mead, methinks,
And through the grasses, here and there,
  A white narcissus winks.

Were Ptolemy alive today,
  And did he know of me,
"Thou art the maestro," he would say,
  "Of all astronomy!"

A thing is sometimes mentioned on account of that which causes it to occur. In the verses I have just cited, I have compared two pairs of things with each other in one and the same stanza, the second of the poem beginning "Those, as they swing their lamps above": this is considered very unusual in poetry. However, I can also quote an even

[1] See *ibid.* pp. 39–41.

more perfect example of virtuosity from my own works—the likening of three, and even four pairs of things in a single stanza; both these feats have been accomplished in the piece here following.

Still yearning, and disquieted,
Still sleepless tossing on his bed,
Wits drunken and disorderly
With the coarse wine of calumny;

He shows to thee in one brief hour
Marvels defeating reason's power—
Now hostile, now the friend sincere,
Now running off, now pressing near;

As if this passion, this reproof,
To be complacent, or aloof,
Were stars conjuring, or in flight,
Fortune's benevolence, or spite.

After so long refusal, he
Took pity on my love, and me,
And I, who envied others' chance,
Am target now for envy's glance.

Together in a garden gay
With bloom we passed our happy day,
The while the bright and whispering flowers
Gave thanks to God for morning's showers:

As if the matin rains, indeed,
The clouds, and that sweet-scented mead,
Were dropping tears, and eyes bedewed,
And cheeks with roses all imbued.

Let none find fault with me or object to my use of the term "conjoining", for those who have knowledge of the stars speak of the meeting of two stars in a single degree as a "conjunction".

I have not yet exhausted my repertoire, but can cite a still more perfect example, the likening of five pairs of things in a single stanza, as in my next quotation.

She sat there privily with me,
And wine besides, to make us three,
While night profound o'ershadowing
Stretched out its long and stealthy wing.

A damsel fair—I would prefer
To die, than not live close with her;
And is it such a dreadful crime
To wish to live this little time?

It was as if myself, and she,
The cup, the wine, the obscurity,
Were earth, and raindrops, and pearls set
Upon a thread, and gold, and jet.

That is a point beyond which it is impossible for anyone to go; neither prosody nor the structure of words will tolerate more than five comparisons in the same stanza.

The writer of these comments and the composer of these verses was far more famous, and in truth gifted, as a theologian and a jurisprudent than as a poet; nevertheless he here hit upon a profound truth about Arabic poetry. To understand what the Arab poet was trying to do, it is necessary to disencumber oneself of the illusion that the poet is a kind of God-given genius, a creature set apart from other men, subject (like the artist and musician of popular imagination) to his own laws. The Arab poet is rather to be considered, and judged, as a craftsman like other craftsmen, a goldsmith of words, a jeweller of verbal images. In my *Anthology of Moorish Poetry* I have tried to explain and illustrate this topic, within the fruitful field of Andalusian verse, and the student is recommended to glance through that book, and in particular the introduction, for a fuller exposition of the variations played by the bards on the old and new themes. For the desert stock of images, astonishingly abundant to be developed out of so barren an environment, received rich reinforcement as the empire spread to embrace fertile valleys, forested plains and wooded heights, broad rivers and tumbling streams, orchards and gardens and the colours and scents of multitudinous flowers, the pale and dusky beauty of Turkish and Ethiop slave-girls, the gold and crimson sunshine of wine.

In the *dolce vita* of sophisticated affluence, the poets developed a kind of drama out of the pleasures and pains of love-making. This drama acquired its stock characters with their stock characterisations: the lover and the beloved of course, and around and between them the confidant, the messenger, the spy, the slanderer, the reproacher. In due course the simple romance became a complicated allegory; the lover was metamorphosed into the poet seeking the prince's favour, his perhaps unattainable beloved; the other figures of the love-drama fitted all too neatly into the changed scenery of court-intrigue. This was followed presently by a further transformation, when the lover became the mystic and the beloved his God; how this new development worked out has been shown in my *Mystical Poems of Ibn al-Fāriḍ* (Dublin, 1956). As that book has now become somewhat rare, it may be useful to repeat here the analysis of how one poet (and he amongst the greatest) treated a range of conventional themes.[1]

(*a*) *Tears of blood.* It is conventionally accepted that lovers weep tears of blood.

(i) I, 11. Sleeplessness has wounded his eyelids, so that the swift-springing tears are mingled all with blood.

(ii) II, 40. Look thou upon a heart that is melted with ardent love for thee, and an eye overwhelmed in the waves of its blood-flecked tears.

(iii) VIII, 22. Surely enough is the blood that has flowed from my wounded eyelids for thee: is this that has come to pass enough for thee?

(iv) IX, 23. A passion had made my blood to flow mid the traces; it ran, a torrent, out of my eyelids, rained o'er the mountain-slope.

(v) XIII, 131. Nay, but my yearning rather is even to run, if so I may, upon an eyelid dabbled with blood, abandoning my feet.

(vi) XIV, 39. I slaughtered the sleep in mine eyelids as hospitality to the ghostly guest, and my tears flowed blood over my cheeks.

(*b*) *Fire and flood.* The poet describes himself as confronted by the double peril of fire (from his burning heart) and flood (from his brimming tears): these two threats sometimes cancel each other out.

(i) II, 5. And ah, my tears that flowed abundantly—but for the hot breaths panting from the fire of yearning, I had scarce escaped from the billows of my weeping.

[1] A full-length exposition of these themes and their elaboration is contained in the second volume of al-Nuwairī, *Nihāyat al-arab*.

(ii) XI, 21. Ye went far from me, and I saw none faithful except my tears, save only a sigh that mounted out of the hot flame of grief.

(iii) XII, 8. For out of my heart springs a flame that serveth well for a firebrand, and from mine eyes stream tears that flood like continuous rains.

(iv) XIV, 24. And naught is the sprinkling shower, but the flow of my tears; and naught the lightning-shaft, but the flaming glow of my sigh.

(*c*) *The lightning smile.* The flashing teeth of the beloved are compared with lightning.

(i) II, 28. And I pity the lightning in its night-courses, pretending to kinship with his mouth, and put to shame by the dazzling gleam of his parted lips.

(ii) VIII, 33–5. How could I forget thee, seeing mine eye, whenever a lightning-flash gleams, turneth eager to meet thee? If thou smilest behind the flash of thy veil, or if thou breathest upon the breeze thy tidings, then I am glad at heart, for the dawn of thy glittering teeth hath shone to mine eyes, and the scent of thy perfume is wafted abroad.

(iii) XIV, 46. The gleam of the lightning over the mountain-folds gave unto us (as bringing to our minds) the flash of thy teeth; and it was the best of gifts.

(*d*) *The invisible lover.* The lover is said to be wasted by grief, to such a point that he vanishes.

(i) II, 6. And welcome to the sickness I suffer on thy account, whereby I have become invisible even to myself: therein stand my proofs before the tribunal of love.

(ii) VII, 21. I concealed my love for you, and pain concealed me, until, by my life, I was well-nigh concealed even from myself.

(iii) IX, 34–5. The substance of all I have encountered and suffered for her (and in my account I have not exceeded due measure, but spoken in summary) is this: I am vanished of wasting, so that my visitor is baffled to find me; and how shall visitors see one who hath not even a shadow?

(iv) XI, 19. I have vanished of wasting even from wasting itself; yea, I have vanished from the cure of my sickness, and the cool waters that would assuage my burning thirst.

(v) XIII, 98. My mightiest yearning hath scraped away my bones, and my body has all perished, but for my two least parts.

(vi) XIV, 19. A lying imagining was the visitation of her image to him who resembled it—not substance of dream or vision.

(vii) XIV, 35. And I have come to a state—because of that wasting which hath not left one spot in me for further mischief—so that my presence is like to my absence to those who visit me.

(*e*) *Glances.* The beloved's glances are compared with arrows or sword-blades, piercing the lover's heart.

(i) III, 13. Refrain—may I have naught of thee!—and reject thou him whose bowels have been mercilessly wounded by wide-eyed enchanters.

(ii) V, 4. O thou who aimest, as one who aimeth the arrows of his glances from the bow of his curved eyebrows, against my bowels to transfix them.

(iii) V, 10. A sword his eyelids draw against my heart, and I see the very languor thereof doth whet its blade.

(iv) VI, 1. Guard thou thy heart if thou passest by Ḥājir, for the gazelles there dwelling have swords flashing in the orbits of their unveiled eyes.

(v) IX, 29. My people know well that I am slain by her glances: for in every limb of her she possesses a whetted point.

(vi) IX, 36. No eye hath alighted on any trace of me, nor have those wide eyes left any remaining mark of me in my passion.

(vii) XIII, 26. The arrow of the clever one of the tribe pierced me, but missed my vitals; the arrow of your glances hath scorched my bowels utterly.

(*f*) *Lips.* The beloved's lips are said to intoxicate, or alternatively to heal, the lover with their saliva.

(i) V, 19–20. Ice-cool are his deep-red lips, and sweet his mouth to kiss in the morning; yea, even before the toothpick's cleansing excelling the musk in fragrance and investing it with its own perfume. Of his mouth and his glances cometh my intoxication; nay, but I see a vintner in his every limb.

(ii) VI, 6. To the crimson of his lips I had recourse again, panting, as I were the thirstiest that ever came down to water, and he denied Euphrates; and none that came up from the water-hole was ever so slaked as I.

(iii) VII, 37. O how lovely is all that he delighteth in! Aye, and how sweet his saliva upon my lips!

(iv) XIII, 29. My sickness cometh from the languor of your eyelids, and my remedy is in the honeyed water of your teeth.

(v) XIII, 51–3. Ah, how I yearn for her radiant face, and how my heart thirsts for these dear red lips! By those lips alike and by her glances I am severally intoxicated: oh joy, for my double intoxication! And I perceive the very wine is inebriated by her lips' breath, and the honey, being confounded, submits to them.

(vi) XIV, 53–4. Is there not any inclination in thee towards showing compassion, and giving up that aversion which made thee turn so cruelly away from one thirsting for the water of thy lips? To moisten the thirsting throat of the sick man at his last gasp, whereby he may regain his health—that were the greatest boon.

The foregoing is but a small fragment of the large lexicon of themes and images which the Arab poet delighted to have by his elbow, or rather by heart. Out of these delicate materials he constructed with infinite patience and skill the arabesque of words and rhythms which it is so great a pleasure for the informed critic to analyse. This, however, was by no means the whole of the story. As if to compensate for the simplification and vocabulary and the abandonment of rare and outlandish words, the Abbasid poets invented a new art, the art of the *badī'*, or rhetorical figures. The morphology of the Arabic language made it comparatively easy to play tricks with words; the poets played this fascinating game to the top of their bent, so that in the end it becomes, truth to tell, somewhat tedious to follow them through the labyrinth of their tortuous inventiveness.[1] Detailed lists of these figures run to great length, and their names vary; here the principal ones only are enumerated, with illustrations drawn again from the poems of Ibn al-Fāriḍ.

(1) *Jinās*. This figure, also called *tajnīs*, consists in using in close proximity two words having the same root letters but with different meanings. It is subdivided into numerous varieties.

(i) *al-mustaufī* (*al-tāmm*): complete correspondence.

ahlan bi-mā lam akun *ahlan* li-mauqi'ihí (II, 43)

(*Welcome* I cry to the hap I was never *worthy* should chance to me.)

[1] For a bibliography, see my *Mystical Poems of Ibn al-Fāriḍ*, p. 16 n. 1.

(ii) *al-mukhtalif* (*al-nāqiṣ*): the two words differ in their vocalisation.

hallā *nahāka nuhāka* 'an laumi mra'in (I, 20)

(Hath not *thy very reason forbidden thee* to reproach a man...?)

(iii) *al-mudhaiyal* (*al-zā'id*): one of the two words has an additional syllable.

fī ḥibbihí bi-lisāni *shākin shākirí* (VI, 16)

(Because he loves the beloved, upon the tongue of *complaint* and *thankfulness* all in one.)

(iv) *al-murakkab*: one of the two elements is made up of two distinct words.

jannatun 'indī rubāhā *amḥalat*
am ḥalat 'ujjiltuhā min jannatai (XIII, 64)

(A garden to me her hills are, whether *they be barren or fair* and fruitful: O may I speedily be brought to this, the first of my two Paradises.)

(v) *al-muṣaḥḥaf*: the two words differ in regard to the diacritical points of certain letters.

wa-'abarta l'ḥajūna wa-*jtazta* fa-*khtar*
-*ta* zdiyāran mashāhida l-autādí (IV, 14)

(And crossest al-Ḥajūn and *passest over*, and *choosest* as thy place of visitation the shrines of the holy saints.)

(vi) *al-muḍāri'* (*al-lāḥiq*): the two words differ only in respect of a single letter.

fa-bi-iqdāmi *raghbatin* ḥīna *yaghshā*
-*ka* bi-iḥjāmi *rahbatin yakhshākā* (VIII, 13)

(So, when *he cometh toward thee*, boldly urged by his *eagerness*, that moment *he dreadeth thee* with all the shrinking of *terror*.)

(vii) *jinās al-ishtiqāq*: two words derived from the same root.

mā-dhā yurīdu l-'*ādhilūna* bi-'*adhli* man
labisa l'khalā'ata wa-*starāḥa* wa-*rāḥā* (III, 16)

(What is it that the *reproachers* desire, in *reproaching* one who has clothed himself in profligacy, and *taken his rest* and *is at repose*?)

(viii) *al-mushābih* (*mimmā yushbih al-mushtaqq*): two words apparently but not actually derived from the same root.

'*utbu* lam *tu'tib* wa-*salmā aslamat*
wa-ḥamā ahlu-ḥimā *ru'yata rai* (XIII, 124)

('*Utbu satisfied* me not, and *Salmā betrayed* me, and the dwellers in the enclosure suffered me not to *look* upon *Rai*.)

(ix) *al-mukhālif* (*al-maqlūb*): two words with identical letters but in a different order.

wa-bi-*ladh'i 'adhlī* lau aṭa'tuka ḍā'irī (VI, 11)

(Yet thou with thy *wounding reproach*, had I obeyed thee, wouldst work me harm.)

(2) *Ṭibāq*. This figure consists in mentioning two words of opposite meanings in the same line.

khairu l-uṣaiḥābi lladhī huwa *āmirī*
bi-l-*ghaiyi* fīhi wa-'an *rashādī zājirí* (VI, 7)

(The best of dear comrades is he, who *commands* me to *stray* for his sake, and *scolds* me away from the *right path* I would have followed.)

(3) *Takāfu'*. Similar to *ṭibāq*, but the opposition between the two words is only metaphorical.

mā *amarra* l-firāqa yā jīrata l-ḥai
-yi wa-*aḥlā* l-talāqi ba'da nfirādí (IV, 18)

(How *bitter* is separation, O neighbours of the sacred quarter, and how *sweet* is reunion after loneliness!)

(4) *Muqābala*. A pair of contrasting ideas elaborated in balanced compound.

minnī lahú dhullu l-khuḍū'i wa-*minhu lī*
'izzu l-manū'i wa-quwwatu l-mustaḍ'ifí (VII, 35)

(*To him I owe* the *humility of submission; his right over me* is the *pride* of *disdainful refusal*, the power of one who despises his victim's impotence.)

(5) *Tarṣī'*. Internal rhymes (*saj'*) exactly corresponding in rhythm.

arbat laṭāfatuhú 'alā nashri l-ṣabā
wa-*abat tarāfatuhu* l-taqammuṣa lādhā (V, 16)

(*Subtler is he* than the exhalation of the sweet East breeze; *he scorns in his luxuriance* to wrap him round even in the finest silks.)

(6) *Muwāzana*. Internal rhymes with the final pair not quite rhyming.

lau tarā aina khamīlātu qubā
wa-*tarā' aina jamīlātu* l-*qubai* (XIII, 74)

(*If thou hadst seen the thickets of Qubā*, and *the lovely maidens* in their *gowns had shown themselves*.)

(7) *Mulā'ama.* Balance between pairs of phrases.

fa-min fu'ādī labībun nāba 'an qabasin
wa-min jufūniya dam'un fāḍa ka-l-diyamí (XII, 8)

(*For out of my heart springs a flame that serveth well for a firebrand, and from mine eyes stream tears that flood like continuous rains.*)

(8) *Radd al-'ajz 'alā l-ṣadr.* The line ends with the same word or phrase as that with which it opens.

yā sākinī l-baṭḥā'i hal min 'audatin
aḥyā bihā *yā sākinī l-baṭḥā'i* (I, 12)

(*O dwellers in the torrent-bed*, is there to be any returning for me, whereby I may live once more, *O dwellers in the torrent-bed*?)

(9) *Ḥusn al-ta'līl.* Ingenious assignment of cause.

lā gharwa an takhadha l-'idhāra ḥamā'ilan
an ẓalla fattākan bihí waqqādhā (V, 12)

(No wonder it is, that he should have taken the hairs upon his cheek to be the suspender-thongs of his sword, seeing that he is ever smiting and slaying therewith.)

(10) *Tajāhul al-'ārif.* Feigned ignorance: the rhetorical question.

a-wamīḍu barqin bi-l-ubairiqi lāḥā
am fī rubā najdin arā miṣbāḥā
am tilka lailā l-'āmirīyatu asfarat
lailan fa-ṣaiyarati l-masā'a ṣabāḥā (III, 1–2)

(Is it a flash of lightning that shone over the mottled mountain, or do I see a lantern flickering in the hills of Nejd? Or is that Lailā of the Banū 'Āmir who unveiled her face at night, and converted the evening dusk into radiant dawn?)

(11) *Mubālagha.* Hyperbole.

'amma shti'ālan khālu wajnatihí akhā
shughulin bihí wajdan abā stinqādhā (V, 18)

(The mole upon his cheek embraces in its conflagration what man soever is passionately occupied with him, and scorneth to seek deliverance.)

(12) *Taḍmīn.* Quoting from the Koran, the Traditions, or a verse of poetry.

ʿanati l-ghazālatu wa-l-ghazālu li-wajhihí
mutalaffitan wa-bihí ʿiyādhan lādhā (v, 15)

(The sun's self, yea, and the graceful gazelle submit humbly (Kor. xx, 110) before his face as he gazes about him, and take refuge and shelter in his beauty.)

fa-l-yaṣnaʿi l-rakbu mā shāʾū bi-anfusihim
humu ahlu badrin fa-lā yakhshauna min ḥarají (II, 38)

(And let the riders do whatsoever they will with themselves, they are the people of Badr, so that they shall fear not for any guilt.[1])

fatkun binā yazdādu minhu muṣauwiran
qatlā musāwira fī banī yazdādhā (v, 11)

(All the more sheds he suddenly our blood, picturing them that Musāwir slew[2] amongst the Banū Yazdādh.)

(13) *Talmīḥ.* Allusion, without direct quotation.

dhū l-fiqāri l-laḥẓu minhā abadan
wa-l-ḥashā minniya ʿamrun wa-ḥuyai (XIII, 54)

(Dhu 'l-Fiqār is ever the cutting glance of her, and my poor heart is as ʿAmr and Ḥuyai.[3])

(14) *al-Laff wa'l-nashr.* Themes are introduced one after the other, and then in turn explained.

fa-ḍuʿfī wa-suqmī dhā ka-ra'yi ʿawādhilī
wa-dhā ka-ḥadīthi l-nafsi ʿankum bi-rajʿatí (XIV, 33)

(So that my weakness and my sickness—the latter is diseased as the judgement of my upbraiders, the former feeble as the whisper within me upon your authority that I shall return to you.)

[1] The reference is to a Tradition (see, e.g. al-Kalābādhī, *al-Taʿarruf*, p. 49) according to which the Prophet promised immunity and Paradise to the heroes of the Battle of Badr.

[2] The poet refers to Musāwir ibn Muḥammad al-Rūmī, the hero whose exploits were celebrated by al-Mutanabbī in two famous odes, one of which served as a model for this poem.

[3] Dhu'l-Fiqār was the name of the sword of ʿAlī ibn Abī Ṭālib; ʿAmr and Ḥuyai the names of two of his victims.

(15) *Īhām.* The *double entendre*, the more remote of the two meanings being the one intended.

kam min faqīrin thamma lā min ja'farin
wāfā l-ajāri'a sā'ilan shaḥḥādhā (v, 29)

(How many a conduit-mouth is there, that has reached to those sandy stretches seeking importunately for water, and of no little rivulet![1])

It has been stated earlier that the length of the formal ode varied from between about a score to a century of couplets; it should now be added that an exceptionally long monorhyme ode, the *Naẓm al-sulūk* of Ibn al-Fāriḍ, extends to as many as 761 *baits*. The possibility of composing even longer poems, reaching in some cases epic proportions, was opened up by the invention of the *muzdawij* form in which "the hemistichs of a poem rhyme together two by two".[2] (This form was the parent of the *mathnawī* which in Persian and Turkish allowed for the full development of epic poetry.) Usually this form was confined to the *rajaz* metre and to didactic verse, such as the well-known *Alfīya* of Ibn Mālik; other uses which may be mentioned are in the versification of the *Kalīla wa-Dimna* composed by Ibn al-Habbārīya (d. 509/1115) entitled *Natā'ij al-fiṭna*, and in a huge biography of the Prophet, *al-Fatḥ al-qarīb fī sīrat al-Ḥabīb*, by Ibn al-Shahīd (d. 793/1391). The really long poem however never came really natural to the Arabs, and the rapid change of rhyme involved has offended their aesthetic taste even down to the present day. In the classical period, the idea of unrhymed verse never arose; in the twentieth century a few experiments have been made in imitation of European models, but "free verse" has appealed more to the modern innovators whose compositions rival in obscurity the most opaque creations that the contemporary West has to offer.

To Moorish Andalusia belongs credit for the discovery and development of strophic verse, notably the *muwashshaḥ* ("the girdled"), an arrangement in four-, five-, or six-line strophes, capable of wide variations in construction and rhyme, a typical scheme being *aa bbbaa*

[1] The commoner meaning of *faqīr* (here "conduit-mouth") is "a poor man"; that of *ja'far* ("little rivulet") the name of Ja'far the Barmecide.

[2] *Encyclopedia of Islam*[1], III, 800.

cccaa, &c., the final *aa* of the last strophe constituting a kind of *envoi*. The causes which led to the development of the strophe in Spain and not in the East are obscure; the influence of popular songs in Romance has long been suspected, and is reinforced by the recent discovery that in the earliest *muwashshaḥs* the *envoi* was actually in Romance. Some part may be due also to the special developments in the West of Arabic music.[1]

In the present selection two *muwashshaḥs* have been included to introduce the student to a particularly attractive variety of Arabic poetry. Needless to say, the novel form became immediately subject to the same conventions of subject-matter, image and rhetorical embellishment as those which governed the more traditional genres.

The present selection concludes with a few poems composed during the nineteenth and twentieth centuries; for a more extensive anthology of contemporary verse, down to about 1950, the student may like to consult my *Modern Arabic Poetry*. There he will encounter a number of examples of strophic poetry, and of other innovations within the field of rhymed and metrical verse. Later, more revolutionary developments yet await systematic study. Amongst the "modern" poems, some interest and even amusement may be stimulated by the formal ode composed in honour of Queen Victoria by that ardent Arab, Christian later turned Muslim, (Aḥmad) Fāris al-Shidyāq. The other specimens suggest the part played by the Arab poet in reviving the memory of the past glories of Islamic civilisation, and as a spokesman for renascent Arab nationalism. The Arab poet's patron was first the tribe, then the caliph, then the sultan, then the king; today it is the nation and the party and, by natural succession, the "leader".

[1] Gibb, *op. cit.* pp. 109–10. For a remarkably ingenious imitation of the technique of the *muwashshaḥ* see *ibid.* pp. 111–12.

TEXTS, TRANSLATIONS AND NOTES

1 AL-SAMAU'AL

1 When a man's honour is not defiled by baseness, then every cloak he cloaks himself in is comely;

2 And if he has never constrained himself to endure despite, then there is no way (for him) to (attain) goodly praise.

3 She (was) reproaching us, that we were few in numbers; so I said to her, "Indeed, noble men are few.

4 Not few are they whose remnants are like to us—youths who have climbed to the heights, and old men (too).

5 It harms us not that we are few, seeing that our kinsman is mighty, whereas the kinsman of the most part of men is abased.

6 We have a mountain where those we protect come to dwell, impregnable, turning back the eye and it a-weary;

7 Its trunk is anchored beneath the soil, and a branch (of it) soars with it to the stars, unattainable, tall.

8 We indeed are a folk who deem not being killed a disgrace, though 'Āmir and Salūl may (so) consider it.

9 The love of death brings our term (of life) near to us, but their term hates death, and is therefore prolonged.

10 Not one sayyid of ours ever died a natural death, nor was any slain of ours ever left where he lay unavenged.

11 Our souls flow out along the edge of the swordblades, and do not flow out along other than the swordblades.

12 We have remained pure and unsullied, and females and stallions who bore us in goodly fame kept intact our stock.

13 We climbed on to the best of backs, and a descending brought us down in due time to the best of bellies.

---

1 Sources: Abū Tammām, *al-Ḥamāsa* (ed. Freytag), 49–54.
J. W. Hirschberg, *Der Dīwān des as-Samau'al ibn 'Adijā'* (Cracow, 1931), 21–3.

Metre: *ṭawīl*.

For a full discussion and analysis of this celebrated poem see Hirschberg, *op. cit.*

2. The usual meaning of *ḍaim* is "wrong, injustice"; here the intention is clearly "being unjust to oneself" in the sense of compelling oneself to endure intolerable hardships.

3. Presumably the taunt was shouted by a woman accompanying into battle the warriors of a rival tribe.

5. "Kinsman": or, "neighbour, protector". See Lane *s.v.* The line may also be construed (with *mā* taken as interrogative) as a question.

١ السموأل بن عادياء

١ إذا المرء لم يَدْنَسْ من اللؤم عِرْضُهُ   فكلُّ رداءٍ يرتديه جميلُ
٢ وإنْ هو لم يَحْمِلْ على النفس ضَيْمَها   فليس إلى حسن الثناء سبيلُ
٣ تُعَيِّرُنا أنّا قليلٌ عديدُنا   فقلتُ لها إنّ الكرام قليلُ
٤ وما قلّ من كانت بقاياه مِثْلَنا   شبابٌ تَسَامَى للعُلا وكهولُ
٥ وما ضَرَّنا أنّا قليلٌ وجارُنا   عزيزٌ وجارُ الأكثرين ذليلُ
٦ لنا جَبَلٌ يحتلّه من نُجيره   منيعٌ يَرُدُّ الطرفَ وهْو كليلُ
٧ رسا أصلُه تحت الثرى وسما به   إلى النجم فرعٌ لا يُنال طويل
٨ وإنّا لَقومٌ ما نرى القتل سُبَّةً   إذا ما رأتْه عامرٌ وسَلُولُ
٩ يُقَرِّبُ حبُّ الموت آجالَنا لنا   وتكرهه آجالُهم فتطول
١٠ وما مات منّا سيّدٌ حَتْفَ أنْفِه   ولا طُلَّ منّا حيث كان قتيل
١١ تسيل على حدّ الظبات نفوسُنا   وليست على غير الظبات تسيل
١٢ صَفَوْنا فلم نكدر وأخلص سرَّنا   إناثٌ أطابت حملَنا وفحول
١٣ عَلَوْنا إلى خير الظهور وحَطَّنا   لوقتٍ إلى خير البطون نُزُول

---

6. The "mountain" is either to be taken metaphorically ("Our glory is so high that its summit cannot be scanned") or literally, as referring to the mountain-fortress of al-Ablaq (al-Fard), the famous redoubt of al-Samau'al.

8. 'Āmir and Salūl are the names of rival tribes; see *Encycl. of Isl.*[2], I, 441–2; *Encycl. of Isl.*[1], IV, 119.

9. Sc. our warriors die young, those of our rivals live on into old age.

11. The commentator al-Tibrīzī explains the second half of this verse as excluding death by the dishonourable instruments of sticks and staves and the like.

12. For this use of *sirr*, see Lane 1338, col. 2.

13. A reference to the loins and wombs of the ancestors of the tribe.

14 So we are as the water of the rain-shower—in our metal is no bluntness, neither is any miser numbered amongst us.

15 We disapprove if we will of what other men say, but they disavow never words spoken by us.

16 Whenever a sayyid of ours disappears, (another) sayyid arises, one eloquent to speak as noble men speak, and strong to act moreover.

17 No fire of ours was ever doused against a night-visitor, neither has any casual guest alighting found fault with us.

18 Our 'days' are famous amongst our foes; they have well-marked blazes and white pasterns;

19 And our swords—in all west and east they have been blunted from smiting against armoured warriors;

20 Their blades are accustomed not to be drawn and then sheathed until the blood of a host is spilled.

21 If you are ignorant, ask the people concerning us and them—and he who knows and he who is ignorant are (assuredly) not equal."

22 Surely the Banu 'l-Daiyān are (as a) pole for their people, their mills turn and rotate around them.

2 AL-NĀBIGHA

1 (News) came to me—may you spurn the curse!—that you had blamed me, and those (things) at which I am full of care and trouble,

2 So I passed the night as if the recurrent thoughts had spread for me a thornbush, wherewith my bed was raised high and disturbed.

---

14. A rain-cloud is a common simile for generosity. "In our metal": lit. "in our stock, handle".

16. For the form *qa'ūlun* see Wright, I, 135B.

17. The poet refers to the Bedouin practice of lighting a fire on the top of the nearest hill to guide night-travellers to the encampment and as a sign that hospitality was to be found there.

18. "Our 'days'": i.e. the famous battles in which the tribe has engaged. The white parts of the noble horse describe the "outstanding" achievements.

20. A *qabīl* is a collection of men descended from various fathers; a *qabīla* is descended all from one father.

22. This verse is assigned by al-Tibrīzī not to al-Samau'al, who was not of the Banu 'l-Daiyān, but to a certain 'Abd al-Malik b. 'Abd al-Raḥīm al-Ḥārithī; see Hirschberg, *op. cit.* 23.

١٤ فنحن كماء المُزْنِ ما فى نِصابنا   كَهامٌ ولا فينا يُعَدُّ بخيل

١٥ ونُنكر إن شئنا على الناس قولَهم   ولا ينكرون القول حين نقول

١٦ إذا سيّدٌ منّا خلا قام سيّدٌ   قَؤُولٌ لما قال الكرامُ فَعُول

١٧ وما أُخْمِدَتْ نارٌ لنا دون طارقٍ   ولا ذمّنا فى النازلين نَزيلُ

١٨ وأيّامُنا مشهورةٌ فى عدوّنا   لها غُرَرٌ معلومةٌ وحُجُولُ

١٩ وأسيافُنا فى كلّ غربٍ ومشرقٍ   بها من قراع الدارعين فلول

٢٠ معوَّدةً أن لا تُسَلَّ نِصالها   فتُغْمَدَ حتّى يُستباحَ قبيلُ

٢١ سَلِي إن جهلتِ الناسَ عنّا وعنهمُ   وليس سواءً عالمٌ وجَهولُ

٢٢ فإنّ بنى الديّان قطبٌ لقومهم   تدور رحاهم حولهم وتجول

٢ النابغة

١ أتانى أبيتَ اللعنَ أنّك لُمْتَنى   وتلك التى أهتمُّ منها وأَنْصَبُ

٢ فبِتُّ كأنّ العائدات فَرَشْنَنِي   هِراسًا به يُعْلَى فراشى ويُقْشَبُ

---

2 Sources: M. Derenbourg, *Le Dîwân de Nâbigha Dhobyânî* (Paris, 1869), 83–4.
W. Ahlwardt, *The Divans of the Six Ancient Arabic Poets* (London, 1870), 4–5.
L. Cheikho, *Shu'arā' al-Naṣrānīya*, 655–6.
Muṣṭafā al-Saqqā, *Mukhtār al-shi'r al-jāhilī* (Cairo, 1368/1948), I, 174–6.
Fu'ād Afrām al-Bustānī, *al-Nābigha al-Dhubyānī* (Beirut, 1950), 11–13.

Metre: *ṭawīl*.

The poem was addressed to al-Nu'mān b. al-Mundhir, last of the Lakhmid rulers of al-Ḥīra (reigned A.D. 580–602).

1. The first hemistich is identical with *v.* 14 of another *qaṣīda* of al-Nābigha, see Cheikho, 688–94. For the formula *abaita 'l-la'na*, see Lane 12, col. 1.

2. "Corrupted": i.e. "made intolerable".

3 I swore—and I left no doubt to your mind—and a man has no recourse beyond God—

4 Surely, if you had been informed of treachery on my part, then your embroidering informant was indeed false and lying.

5 But I was a man who had an ample part of the earth where I might roam at will and betake myself,

6 Kings and brothers—whenever I came to them I would be given control of their wealth and advanced in favour—

7 Just as you do with regard to a people I have seen you take as your intimates, not considering them to have sinned in the matter of gratitude.

8 For you are (as) a sun, and the (other) kings are stars; when (your sun) rises, not one star appears from amongst them.

9 So do not leave me with a threat, as though I were to other men (as) one smeared with pitch, a scabby (camel).

10 Do you not see that God has given you great might, (so that) you see every king quivering before it?

11 You are not one to spare a brother whose disordered state you have not repaired. Who is the (truly) polished man?

12 So if I am wronged, yet I am a slave whom you have wronged; and if you are a complacent man, then the like of you is apt to be complacent.

3 'ANTARA

1 Make war on me, O vicissitudes of the nights, (now) on my right hand and now on my left,

2 And labour to be hostile to me and to thwart me; by Allah! you have never occupied my mind.

---

4. For the construction with *la-* introducing the complement of an oath, see Wright, II, 19B, 175D.

6. The reference is to the Ghassānid rulers who had previously patronised the poet.

7. "In the matter of gratitude": sc. towards their former patrons.

8. The order is that given by al-Saqqā; the other editors transfer this verse to follow *v.* 10. For *fa-innaka* Derenbourg and Ahlwardt read *bi-annaka*.

9. "A scabby (camel)": i.e. to be avoided like the plague.

10. "Great might": reading *sauratan*. The variants *sūratan* ("rank, dignity") and *ṣūratan* ("beauty of form") are also quoted.

٣ حلفتُ فلم أترك لنفسك ريبةً — وليس وراء اللّه للمرء مَذْهَبُ

٤ لئن كنتُ قد بُلّغْتَ عنّى خيانةً — لَمُبْلِغُك الواشى أَغَشُّ وأَكْذَبُ

٥ ولكنّنى كنتُ آمرءًا لِىَ جانبٌ — من الأرض فيه مستراد ومَذْهَبُ

٦ ملوكٌ وإخوانٌ إذا ما أتيتُهم — أُحَكَّمُ فى أموالهم وأُقَرَّبُ

٧ كفعلك فى قومٍ أراك اصطنعتَهم — فلم تَرَهُمْ فى شكر ذلك أَذْنَبُوا

٨ فإنّك شمسٌ والملوكُ كواكبٌ — إذا طلعتْ لم يبدُ منهنّ كَوْكَبُ

٩ فلا تتركنّى بالوعيد كأنّنى — إلى الناس مَطْلِىٌّ به القارُ أَجْرَبُ

١٠ ألم تر أن اللّه أعطاك سورةً — ترى كلّ مَلْكٍ دونها يَتَذَبْذَبُ

١١ ولستَ بمُسْتَبْقٍ أخًا لا تَلُمُّه — على شَعَثٍ أىُّ الرجال المُهَذَّبُ

١٢ فإن أكُ مظلومًا فعبدٌ ظلمتَه — وإن تك ذا عُتْبَى فمثلك يُعْتِبُ

٣ عنترة

١ حَارِبِينى يا نائباتِ الليالى — عن يمينى وتارةً عن شمالى

٢ وٱجهدى فى عداوتى وعنادى — أنتِ واللّه لم تُلِمّى ببالى

---

11. Sc. "You are not the man to leave a rebel untamed or unpunished." The original meaning of *muhadhdhab* (now "cultured") is "trimmed" (of an arrow).

12. "If you are complacent": i.e. "inclined to overlook an offence".

3 Source: Cheikho, 862–3.
Metre: *khafīf*.
This poem, though in the spirit of ʻAntara, is of very doubtful authenticity; it is not included in Ahlwardt's *Divans* or al-Bustānī's selections (Beirut, 1955).

3 I have a high purpose firmer than a rock and stronger than immovable mountains,

4 And a sword which, when I strike with it ever, the useless spear-heads give way before it,

5 And a lance-point which, whenever I lose my way in the night, guides me and restores me from straying,

6 And a mettlesome steed that never sped, but that the lightning trailed behind it from the striking of its hooves.

7 Dark of hue (it is), splitting the starless night with a blackness, between its eyes a blaze like the crescent moon,

8 Ransoming me with its own life, and I ransom it with my life, on the day of battle, and (with) my wealth.

9 And whenever the market of the war of the tall lances is afoot, and it blazes with the polished, whetted blades,

10 I am the broker thereof, and my spear-point is a merchant purchasing precious souls.

11 Wild beasts of the wilderness, when war breaks into flame, follow me from the empty wastes;

12 Follow me, (and) you will see the blood of the foemen streaming between the hillocks and the sands.

13 Then return thereafter, and thank me, and remember what you have seen of my deeds,

14 And take sustenance of the skulls of the people for your little children and your whelps.

---

4. "The useless spear-heads": this seems to be the meaning. For *qurūn* in this sense, see Lane 2091, col. 1. Possibly *khawālī* is to be taken as from the root KHLY ("cutting") rather than KHLW ("empty"). For the adverbial *al-dahra*, see Lane 923, col. 3. Note the *jinās al-ishtiqāq* between *takhallat* and *'l-khawālī*.

٣ إنّ لى همّةً أشدَّ من الصخـ ـرِ وأقْوَى من راسيات الجبال

٤ وحسامًا إذا ضربتُ به الدهـ ـرَ تخلّتْ عنه القرون الخوالى

٥ وسنانًا إذا تعسّفتُ فى الليـ ـل هدانى وردّنى عن ضلالى

٦ وجوادًا ما سار إلّا سرى البر قُ وراه من ٱقتداح النعال

٧ أدهمٌ يصدع الدجى بسواد بين عينيه غرّةٌ كالهلال

٨ يفتدينى بنفسه وأُفَدّيـ ـه بنفسى يوم القتال ومالى

٩ وإذا قام سوقُ حرب العوالى وتلظّى بالمُرْهَفات الصقال

١٠ كنتُ دلّالها وكان سنانى تاجرًا يشترى النفوسَ الغوالى

١١ يا سباعَ الفلا إذا ٱشتعل الحر بُ ٱتبعينى من القفار الخوالى

١٢ اِتبعينى ترى دماء الأعادى سائلاتٍ بين الربى والرمال

١٣ ثم عودى من بعد ذا وٱشكرينى وٱذكرى ما رأيتِه من فعالى

١٤ وخذى من جماجم القوم قوتاً لبنيك الصغار والأشبال

---

7. Note the *ṭibāq* between *bi-sawādin* and *ghurratun*.
12. *Sāʾilātin* is plural in concord with *dimāʾa*, pl. of *damun*.

4 AL-KHANSĀ'

1 I was sleepless, and I passed the night keeping vigil, as if my eyes had been anointed with pus,

2 Watching the stars—and I had not been charged to watch them—and anon wrapping myself in the ends of ragged robes.

3 For I had heard—and it was not news to rejoice me—one making report, who had come repeating intelligence,

4 Saying, "Ṣakhr is dwelling there in a tomb, struck to the ground beside the grave, between certain stones".

5 Depart then, and may God not keep you far (from Him), being a man who eschewed injustice, and ever sought after bloodwit.

6 You used to carry a heart that brooked no wrong, compounded in a nature that was never cowardly,

7 Like the spear-point whose (bright) shape lights up the night, (a man) bitter in resolution, free and the son of free-men.

8 So I shall weep for you, so long as ringdove laments and the night stars shine for the night-traveller,

9 And I shall never make my peace with a people with whom you were at war, not till the black cooking-pot of the (good) host becomes white!

---

4 Sources: al-Buḥturī, *Kitāb al-Ḥamāsa* (Beirut, 1910), 271–2.
Anīs al-julasā' fī Dīwān al-Khansā' (Beirut, 1888), 33–5.
L. Cheikho, *Commentaires sur le Diwan d'al-Ḫansā'* (Beirut, 1896), 109–18.

Metre: *basīṭ*.

This poem is one of a set composed by al-Khansā' on the death of her brother Ṣakhr. The version here printed is that given by al-Buḥturī; in the editions of the *Dīwān* the following opening couplet is prefixed:

yā 'aini jūdī bi-dam'in minka mighrāri
wa-bkī li-Ṣakhrin bi-dam'in minka midrāri

1. "Anointed with pus": sc. painful with the matter exuded by ophthalmia.

2. "Watching the stars" was a common description of sleeplessness. The poetess rebuts the notion that she was appointed nightwatchman over the flocks and the encampment.

٤ الخنساء

١ إِنِّى أَرِقْتُ فَبِتُّ ٱللَّيْلَ سَاهِرَةً   كَأَنَّمَا كُحِلَتْ عَيْنِى بِعُوَّارِ

٢ أَرْعَى ٱلنُّجُومَ وَمَا كُلِّفْتُ رِعْيَتَهَا   وَتَارَةً أَتَغَشَّى فَضْلَ أَطْمَارِ

٣ وَقَدْ سَمِعْتُ وَلَمْ أَبْجَحْ بِهِ خَبَرًا   مُحَدِّثًا جَاءَ يَنْمِى رَجْعَ أَخْبَارِ

٤ يَقُولُ صَخْرٌ مُقِيمٌ ثَمَّ فِى جَدَثٍ   لَدَى ٱلضَّرِيحِ صَرِيعٌ بَيْنَ أَحْجَارِ

٥ فَٱذْهَبْ فَلَا يُبْعِدَنْكَ ٱللّٰهُ مِنْ رَجُلٍ   تَرَّاكِ ضَيْمٍ وَطَلَّابٍ بِأَوْتَارِ

٦ قَدْ كُنْتَ تَحْمِلُ قَلْبًا غَيْرَ مُهْتَضَمٍ   مُرَكَّبًا فِى نِصَابٍ غَيْرِ خَوَّارِ

٧ مِثْلَ ٱلسِّنَانِ تُضِىءُ ٱللَّيْلَ صُورَتُهُ   مُرُّ ٱلْمَرِيرَةِ حُرٌّ وَٱبْنُ أَحْرَارِ

٨ فَسَوْفَ أَبْكِيكَ مَا نَاحَتْ مُطَوَّقَةٌ   وَمَا أَضَاءَتْ نُجُومُ ٱللَّيْلِ لِلسَّارِى

٩ وَلَنْ أُصَالِحَ قَوْمًا كُنْتَ حَرْبَهُمُ   حَتَّى تَعُودَ بَيَاضًا جُؤْنَةُ ٱلْقَارِ

---

3. *Anīs* reads *abhaj* for *abjaḥ*, *mukhabbirin* for *muḥaddithin*, and *qāma* for *jā'a*.

4. *Anīs* reads this couplet as follows:

qāla bnu ummiki thāwin bi-l-ḍarīḥi wa-qad
sawwū 'alaihi bi-alwāḥin wa-aḥjāri

5. For *min rajulin* as *tamyīz*, see Wright, II, 138B. For *tarrāki* Cheikho reads *darrāki*, *Anīs* gives *mannā'i*.

7. *Anīs* reads *jaldu* for *murru*.

8. For *fa-saufa* Cheikho and *Anīs* read *wa-saufa*.

9. For *uṣāliḥa* Cheikho and *Anīs* read *usālima*. Both Cheikho and *Anīs* print additional verses following this couplet.

5 'UMAR IBN ABĪ RABĪ'A

1 Would that Hind had fulfilled to us her promise, and healed our souls of their suffering!

2 Would that she had acted independently for once! It is the weakling who does not act independently.

3 They asserted that she asked our lady-neighbours, when she stripped herself one day to bathe,

4 "Do you see me to be as he describes me—in God's name answer truly!—or does he not observe moderation?"

5 Then they laughed together, saying to her, "Fair in every eye is the one you love!"

6 (So they spoke) out of an envy with which they were charged because of her; and of old envy has existed amongst men.

7 A young maiden (is she) who, when she discloses her cool lips, there is revealed from them (teeth white as) camomile-blossoms or hailstones.

8 She has two eyes whose lids contain an intense whiteness and blackness, and in her neck is a slender softness.

9 Tender is she, cool in the season of heat when the vehemence of the summer has burst into flame,

10 Warm in the wintertime, a coverlet for a lad under the night when the bitter cold wraps him around.

11 Well I remember when I spoke to her, the tears running down over my cheek,

---

5 Sources: *Dīwān* (Beirut, 1380/1961), 101–2.
Aḥmad Amīn and others, *al-Muntakhab*, I, 74–6.
al-Aghānī, I, 22 (verse 1), V, 75 (verses 1–6).

Metre: *ramal*.

1. Hind is one of the ladies frequently mentioned by 'Umar ibn Abī Rabī'a (*Aghānī*, I, 67, 141; XIX, 55, 56), perhaps to be identified with Hind bint al-Ḥārith of the Banū Murra (*Aghānī*, I, 73–6). For the construction *laita Hindan* see Lane 2683; Wright, II, 82 C.

2. The poet wishes that Hind had disregarded the critics and declared her love openly.

3. *Aghānī*, V, 75 gives the variant reading *wa-la-qad qālat li-jārātin lahā dhāta yaumin wa-ta'arrat tabtarid* which gives the same meaning.

٥ عمر بن أبى ربيعة

١ لَيْتَ هِنْدًا أَنْجَزَتْنَا مَا تَعِدْ وَشَفَتْ أَنْفُسَنَا مِمَّا تَجِدْ

٢ وَٱسْتَبَدَّتْ مَرَّةً وَاحِدَةً إِنَّمَا ٱلْعَاجِزُ مَنْ لَا يَسْتَبِدْ

٣ زَعَمُوهَا سَأَلَتْ جَارَتَنَا وَتَعَرَّتْ ذَاتَ يَوْمٍ تَبْتَرِدْ

٤ أَكَمَا يَنْعَتُنِي تُبْصِرْنَنِي عَمْرَكُنَّ ٱللَّهَ أَمْ لَا يَقْتَصِدْ

٥ فَتَضَاحَكْنَ وَقَدْ قُلْنَ لَهَا حَسَنٌ فِي كُلِّ عَيْنٍ مَنْ تَوَدْ

٦ حَسَدًا حُمِّلْنَهُ مِنْ أَجْلِهَا وَقَدِيمًا كَانَ فِي ٱلنَّاسِ ٱلْحَسَدْ

٧ غَادَةٌ يَفْتَرُّ عَنْ أَشْنَبِهَا حِينَ تَجْلُوهُ أَقَاحٍ أَوْ بَرَدْ

٨ وَلَهَا عَيْنَانِ فِي طَرْفَيْهِمَا حَوَرٌ مِنْهَا وَفِي ٱلْجِيدِ غَيَدْ

٩ طَفْلَةٌ بَارِدَةُ ٱلْقَيْظِ إِذَا مَعْمَعَانُ ٱلصَّيْفِ أَضْحَى يَتَّقِدْ

١٠ سُخْنَةُ ٱلْمَشْتَى لِحَافٌ لِلْفَتَى تَحْتَ لَيْلٍ حِينَ يَغْشَاهُ ٱلصَّرَدْ

١١ وَلَقَدْ أَذْكُرُ إِذْ قُلْتُ لَهَا وَدُمُوعِي فَوْقَ خَدِّي تَطَّرِدْ

---

4. For the construction *'amrakunna 'llāha* see Lane 2155, and the alternative explanations there given.

6. For *ḥasadan* (accusative of *ḥāl*) the Beirut edition reads *ḥasadun*.

7. *Ashnabu* is an adjective ("lips" or "mouth" or "front-teeth" to be understood) meaning "lustrous, cool, sweet, delicate". In *al-Muntakhab* the reading *taftarru* is preferred, but the masculine form is more chaste with the verb so far separated from its (feminine) subject. *Aqāḥin* is plural of *quḥwān* (*uqḥuwān*).

8. *Ḥawarun* signifies "intense blackness of the pupils and whiteness of the surrounding parts of the eyes".

9. This and the following verse are omitted in *al-Muntakhab*.

10. "A coverlet for a lad": perhaps a playful reference to Koran, II, 183, where husband and wife are said to be a *libāsun* for each other.

11. For *qad* with the imperfect see Lane 2491; Wright, I, 286C.

12 I said, "Who are you?" She answered, "I am one emaciated by passion, worn out by sorrow.

13 We are the people of al-Khaif, of the people of Minā; for any slain by us there is no retaliation."

14 I said, "Welcome! You are (the goal of) our desire. Name yourselves now!" She said, "I am Hind.

15 My heart is destroyed (by grief), and it yet comprehends (a youth slim as) a straight, true lance, (clad) in fine raiment.

16 Your people are indeed neighbours of ours; we and they are but a single thing!"

17 They told me that she bewitched me—how excellent is that bewitchment!

18 Whenever I said, "When shall be our tryst?" Hind would laugh and say, "After tomorrow!"

6 BASHSHĀR IBN BURD

1 Long has grown my night through the love of one who I think will not draw near me.

2 Never, so long as the light of the stars appears to your eyes

3 Or singing-girl chants an ode in the presence of a tippler,

4 Will I have found consolation for ʿAbda, love so overwhelms me.

5 If her love were for sale, I would purchase it with (many) properties,

6 And were it in my power, willingly (in the vicissitudes of affairs)

7 Would I ransom her from death with everything I possess.

---

12. Hind describes herself in the conventional manner of the lovelorn.

13. Al-Khaif is the summit of Minā near Mecca, see Yāqūt, III, 499–500. For the part played by Minā in the Mecca Pilgrimage see *E.I.* III, 498–9: "all Minā is a place of sacrifice", so that the lover "slain" there by the beauty of the beloved is to be accounted a sacrifice and therefore not covered by the laws of retaliation.

15. For *khubbila* the reading *ḍullila* is given in *al-Muntakhab*. *Sābirī* is derived from Sābūr (Shāpūr), see Lane *s.v.*

17. "Bewitched me": for the "blowing on knots" practised by enchantresses see Koran, CXIII, 4.

١٢ قُلْتُ مَنْ أَنْتِ فَقَالَتْ أَنَا مَنْ   شَفَّهُ ٱلْوَجْدُ وَأَبْلاهُ ٱلْكَمَدْ
١٣ نَحْنُ أَهْلُ ٱلْخَيْفِ مِنْ أَهْلِ مِنًى   مَا لِمَقْتُولٍ قَتَلْنَاهُ قَوَدْ
١٤ قُلْتُ أَهْلاً أَنْتُمُ بُغْيَتُنَا   فَتَسَمَّيْنَ فَقَالَتْ أَنَا هِنْدْ
١٥ إِنَّمَا خَبَّلَ قَلْبِي فَٱحْتَوَى   صَعْدَةً فِي سَابِرِيٍّ تَطَّرِدْ
١٦ إِنَّمَا أَهْلُكِ جِيرَانٌ لَنَا   إِنَّمَا نَحْنُ وَهُمْ شَيْءٌ أَحَدْ
١٧ حَدَّثُونِي أَنَّهَا لِي نَفَثَتْ   عُقَداً يَا حَبَّذَا تِلْكَ ٱلْعُقَدْ
١٨ كُلَّمَا قُلْتُ مَتَى مِيعَادُنَا   ضَحِكَتْ هِنْدٌ وَقَالَتْ بَعْدَ غَدْ

٦ بشّار بن برد

١ طال لَيْلِي مِن حُبِّ مَن   لا أُراه مقاربي
٢ أبدًا ما بدا لعيـ   نك ضوء الكواكب
٣ أو تغنّت قصيدةً   قينةٌ عند شارب
٤ فتعزّيتُ عن عُبَيْـ   دةَ والحبُّ غالبي
٥ تلك لو بيع حبُّها اَبْـ   تَعْتُه بالحرائب
٦ ولَوِ اسطعتُ طائعًا   في الأمور النوائب
٧ لفداها من الردى   هاربي بعد قاربي

---

6 Source: *Dīwān* (Cairo, 1369/1950), I, 163–4.
Metre: *khafīf*.
2. Partial *jinās* between *abadan* and *badā*.
3. Alliteration in this and the following line.
6. Note *jinās al-ishtiqāq*.
7. "With everything I possess": for the idiom, see Lane 2889, col. 3.

8 My beloved reproached (me)—and the lover abounds in reproaches—

9 Because of a tale that the words of a liar carried to her.

10 So I tossed sleeplessly, my locks disarrayed,

11 Marvelling at her repelling (me)—and passion abounds in marvels—

12 And I said, with tears covering my breast-bones,

13 "If despair for 'Abda appears, then my bewailer has already arisen."

14 O 'Abda, for God's sake set free from constant torment

15 A man who, before you (came on the scene), was a monk, or like a monk,

16 Keeping vigil all the night, considering the consequences.

17 Then passion for a ripe wench deflected him from worship,

18 (A girl) the love of whom preoccupied him from the reckoning of the Reckoner,

19 A lover, whose heart will never repent of yearning for her,

20 Suffering in his heart as (if) of the bite of scorpions.

21 Even so the lover advances the mention of the beloved ones.

22 And I feared lest my kinsmen should carry out my bier

23 (All too) hastily, ere I should see in you any kindliness.

24 So when you hear one of my kinswomen weeping,

25 Mourning, amid the black-robed women, one slain by ripe wenches,

26 Then know that it was the love of you that led me to destruction.

---

13. "Then my bewailer": sc. I am as good as dead already.
15. The poet puts on the pose of an early ascetic, imitating the ways of Christian monks.

٨ عتبتْ خُلّتى وذُو ال — حُبِّ جَمُّ المعاتب
٩ من حديث نَمَى الي — ها به قولُ كاذب
١٠ فتقلّبتُ ساهرًا — مقشعرَّ الذوائب
١١ عجباً من صدودها — والهوى ذو عجائب
١٢ ولقد قلتُ والدمو — عُ لباسُ الترائب
١٣ لو بدا اليأسُ من عبي — دة قد قام نادبى
١٤ عَبْدَ باللّه أطْلِقى — من عذابٍ مواصب
١٥ رجلاً كان قبلكم — راهباً أو كراهب
١٦ يسهو الليلَ كلّه — نَظَراً فى العواقب
١٧ فثناه عن العبا — دةِ وَجْدٌ بكاعب
١٨ شغلتْه بحبّها — عن حساب المحاسب
١٩ عاشق ليس قلبُه — من هواها بتائب
٢٠ يشتكى من فؤاده — مِثْلَ لَسْع العقارب
٢١ وكذاك المحبُّ يَلْ — قى بذكر الحبائب
٢٢ ولقد خفتُ أن يرو — حَ بنعشى أقاربى
٢٣ عاجلاً قبل أن أرى — فيكمُ لين جانب
٢٤ فإذا ما سمعتِ با — كيةً من قرائبى
٢٥ ندبتْ فى المسلّبا — ت قتيلَ الكواعب
٢٦ فاعلمى أنّ حبّكم — قادنى للمعاطب

---

16. "The consequences": i.e. of sins.
18. "The Reckoner": Allah, on the Day of Judgement.

7 ABŪ NUWĀS

1 The man burdened with passion is a weary man, deep emotion unsteadies him.

2 If he weeps, it is right that he should; what he is charged with is no joke.

3 Whensoever one cause (of my pains) comes to an end, (another) cause returns from you to me.

4 You are laughing lightheartedly, whilst the lover bursts into tears.

5 You marvel at my sickness; that I am hale and hearty—that is the (true) marvel.

8 ABU 'L-'ATĀHIYA

1 Alas for the (all too) short time passed between al-Khawarnaq and as-Sadīr

2 When we (were esconced) in apartments of Paradise, swimming in the sea of joy,

3 In (a party of) youths who possessed the reins of Time, (youths) like to falcons,

4 Not (one) of them but he that was bold to (gratify) passion, not self-restrained,

---

7 Sources: The poem is given in the *Dīwān* of Abū Nuwās (ed. Aḥmad 'Abd al-Majīd al-Ghazālī, Cairo, 1935), 227.
al-Muntakhab, I, 107–8.
Ibn Khallikān, *loc. cit.*, states that it was the first poem composed by Abū Nuwās.

Metre: *muqtaḍab*.

Figures. Note *ṭibāq* in verse 1 (*ḥāmilu* and *yastakhiffuhu*, *ta'ibu* and *al-ṭarabu*), in verse 3 (*inqaḍā* and *'āda*), in verse 4 (*taḍḥakīna* and *yantaḥibu*) and verse 5 (*saqamī* and *ṣiḥḥatī*).

1. The second half of the couplet is to be construed as a *ḥāl* qualifying *ta'ibu*. The editors of *al-Muntakhab* appear to gloss *al-ṭarabu* by *al-ghinā'* (i.e. "song, music"), and they paraphrase "induces him to unrestraint". For the connection between *ṭarab* and *khiffa* however see Lane 1835–6; *ṭarab* can mean "grief" as well as "joy"; its use in the sense of "music" is post-classical, see Dozy, II, 29.

2. In 'Abd al-Ḥamīd's edition of Ibn Khallikān (Cairo, 1367/1948), I, 374, the variant reading *fa-ḥaqqa* for *yaḥiqqu* is noted, overcoming the grammatical irregu-

٧ أبو نواس

١ حَامِلُ ٱلْهَوَى تَعِبُ   يَسْتَخِفُّهُ ٱلطَّرَبُ
٢ إِنْ بَكَى يَحِقُّ لَهُ   لَيْسَ مَا بِهِ لَعِبُ
٣ كُلَّمَا ٱنْقَضَى سَبَبٌ   مِنْكِ عَادَ لِى سَبَبُ
٤ تَضْحَكِينَ لَاهِيَةً   وَٱلْمُحِبُّ يَنْتَحِبُ
٥ تَعْجَبِينَ مِنْ سَقَمِى   صِحَّتِى هِىَ ٱلْعَجَبُ

٨ أبو العتاهية

١ لَهْفِى عَلَى ٱلزَّمَنِ ٱلْقَصِيرِ   بَيْنَ ٱلْخَوَرْنَقِ وَٱلسَّدِيرِ
٢ إِذْ نَحْنُ فِى غُرَفِ ٱلْجِنَا   نِ نَعُومُ فِى بَحْرِ ٱلسُّرُورِ
٣ فِى فِتْيَةٍ مَلَكُوا عِنَا   نَ ٱلدَّهْرِ أَمْثَالِ ٱلصُّقُورِ
٤ مَا مِنْهُمُ إِلَّا ٱلْجَسُو   رُ عَلَى ٱلْهَوَى غَيْرُ ٱلْحَصُورِ

---

larity of an imperfect following a perfect in the apodosis of a conditional sentence.

3. After the general opening statement, the poet turns to address the lady of his affection and sorrow. With *sabab* one is to understand some such word as *ālāmī*.

8 Sources: *Al-Aghānī*, III, 156–7.
Dīwān (Beirut, 1900), 311–12 (verses 1, 2, 18–23).
al-Muntakhab, I, 112–13 (verses 1–11).
Shauqī Ḍaif, *al-Fann*, 77–8 (verses 1–16).

Metre: *kāmil* (*majzū'*).

1. Al-Khawarnaq and al-Sadīr were palaces outside ancient Ḥīra of the last Lakhmid "king" al-Nu'mān ibn al-Mundhir (d. *ca.* A.D. 602). The poet laments in Jāhilī fashion the ruins of a former "encampment".

2. The word *ghuraf* is used for the "apartments" of Paradise in Koran, XXIX, 58; XXXIX, 21.

4. The word *ḥaṣūr* also connotes "impotent".

5 Passing from hand to hand a crimson wine, of the choicest pressing of the grape,

6 A virgin (wine), nurtured by the rays of the sun in the heat of the noonday,

7 Never brought near to fire, unsullied by the cauldron's grease,

8 And (here and there) a tunic-robed (lad) going before the people like a shy fawn,

9 Bearing a glass extracting the subtlest secret from the mind,

10 Bright as a pearly star in the hand of the circulator,

11 Leaving the noble man unaware of what (is) before from (what is) behind;

12 And slender-waisted (maidens) would visit us after the rest from (their) chambers,

13 Plump their buttocks, wearing rings upon their waists,

14 Shining their faces, closely veiled, restraining their glances, dark-eyed,

15 Luxuriating in (heavenly) bliss, drenched in ambergris,

16 Sweeping along in the robes of (their) charms, and undergarments, and silk,

17 Never seeing the sun save as a pendant (glimpsed) through the gaps of (their) curtains.

18 And with God's trusty (vicar) we take refuge from stumbling Time

19 And to (come to) him we have wearied our riding beasts, (urged on) evening and morning,

---

5. "Choicest": lit. "fresh milking".

6. *Tudna*: the *Muntakhab* editors read *tadnu* "has not drawn near".

8. For *wāw* with the sense of *rubba* see Wright, II, 216 D. The *qurtaq* (from Persian *kurta*) was a tunic or short jacket.

10. The phrase *al-kaukab al-durrī* (in association with *zujāja* in verse 9) echoes Koran, XXIV, 35, a particularly impudent parodying of the much-revered "Light-Verse".

13. *Raiyā* is fem. of *raiyān* from RWY. *Rawādif* (sing. *rādifa*) means orig. "layers of fat in the hinder part of a camel's hump" (Lane 1068); it is cognate with *ridf* (pl. *ardāf*) = "buttock".

14. "Restraining their glances": a reminiscence of Koran, XXXVII, 47; XXXVIII, 52; LV, 56. The girls are fondly compared with houris of Paradise.

٥ يَتَعَاوَرُونَ مُدَامَةً   صَهْبَاءَ مِنْ حَلَبِ ٱلْعَصِيرِ
٦ عَذْرَاءَ رَبَّاهَا شُعَا   عُ ٱلشَّمْسِ فِي حَرِّ ٱلْهَجِيرِ
٧ لَمْ تُدْنَ مِنْ نَارٍ وَلَمْ   يَعْلَقْ بِهَا وَضَرُ ٱلْقُدُورِ
٨ وَمُقَرْطَقٍ يَمْشِى أَمَا   مَ ٱلْقَوْمِ كَالرَّشَأِ ٱلْغَرِيرِ
٩ بِزُجَاجَةٍ تَسْتَخْرِجُ ٱلْ   سِّرَّ ٱلدَّقِيقَ مِنَ ٱلضَّمِيرِ
١٠ زَهْرَاءَ مِثْلِ ٱلْكَوْكَبِ ٱلْ   دُّرِّيِّ فِى كَفِّ ٱلْمُدِيرِ
١١ تَدَعُ ٱلْكَرِيمَ وَلَيْسَ يَدْ   رِى مَا قَبِيلٌ مِنْ دَبِيرِ
١٢ وَمُخَصَّرَاتٍ زُرْنَنَا   بَعْدَ ٱلْهُدُوءِ مِنَ ٱلْخُدُورِ
١٣ رَيَّا رَوَادِفُهُنَّ يَلْ   بَسْنَ ٱلْخَوَاتِمَ فِى ٱلْخُصُورِ
١٤ غُرِّ ٱلْوُجُوهِ مُحَجَّبَا   تٍ قَاصِرَاتِ ٱلطَّرْفِ حُورِ
١٥ مُتَنَعِّمَاتٍ فِى ٱلنَّعِيـ   ـمِ مُضَمَّخَاتٍ بِٱلْعَبِيرِ
١٦ يَرْفُلْنَ فِى حُلَلِ ٱلْمَحَا   سِنِ وَٱلْمَجَاسِدِ وَٱلْحَرِيرِ
١٧ مَا إِنْ يَرَيْنَ ٱلشَّمْسَ إِ   لَّا ٱلْقُرْطَ مِنْ خَلَلِ ٱلسُّتُورِ
١٨ وَإِلَى أَمِينِ ٱللّٰهِ مَهْ   رَبُنَا مِنَ ٱلدَّهْرِ ٱلْعَثُورِ
١٩ وَإِلَيْهِ أَتْعَبْنَا ٱلْمَطَا   يَا بِٱلرَّوَاحِ وَبِٱلْبُكُورِ

---

15. The comparison with Paradise (*naʿīm*) is continued.

16. The ladies are triply robed in their natural charms (*maḥāsin*), their underclothes (*majāsid*) and their silk gowns.

17. For the construction *mā in* see Wright, I, 284D; II, 301B. The word *qurṭ* ("ear-drop") is also used metaphorically of the Pleiades (Lane 2517) with whose fainter radiance the sun's burning light is compared as seen through the lattices of the women's apartments.

18. The poet has completed his *nasīb* and now turns to the main subject of his poem, the panegyric following the description of the journey, both topics here much abbreviated. "God's trusty vicar" is the caliph al-Hādī (169–70/785–6) for whom the poem was composed.

20 Their cheeks twisted (with pride), as if winged with the wings of eagles,

21 Garmented in darkness, (faring) over smooth (plain) and rugged (height)

22 Until they brought us at last to the lord of cities and palaces

23 Who even before (his) weaning was (wise) as of the age of a mature and (grave) elder.

9 ABŪ TAMMĀM

1 The sword is truer in tidings than (any) writings: in its edge is the boundary between earnestness and sport.

2 (Swords) white as to their blades, not (books) black as to their pages—in their broad sides (texts) lies the removing of doubt and uncertainties;

3 And knowledge (resides) in the flames of the lances flashing between the two massed armies, not in the seven luminaries.

4 Where (now) is the recital (of the astrologers), indeed where are the stars, and the embroidery and the lie they fashioned concerning them?—

5 (Mere) forgery and concocted stories, not to be reckoned either (firm-rooted) mountain-tree or (even river-fringing) willow,

6 Marvels they alleged the days would reveal in (portentous) Ṣafar or Rajab,

---

21. The horses are black, or in black trappings, the colour of the Abbasids.

9 Sources: *Dīwān*, with commentary of al-Tibrīzī (ed. 'Abd al-Wahhāb 'Azzām, Cairo, 1951–7), I, 45–79.
al-Muntakhab, II, 222–9.

Metre: *basīṭ*.

This poem celebrates the capture in 223/838 of the Byzantine fortress-city of 'Ammūriya (Amorium) by al-Mu'taṣim. The astrologers had warned the caliph against attempting its assault at that time, but he ignored their advice. The Byzantines are said to have written to him that "they found it in their books that their city would not be taken save in the time when the figs and grapes were ripe" (see *v.* 59). That would not happen for several months yet, and "in the present season of cold the caliph could not tarry there".

1. Note the *jinās* (*tāmm*) between the two meanings of *ḥadd*, the *jinās* (*lāḥiq*) between *ḥadd* and *jidd*, and the *ṭibāq* between *jidd* and *la'ib*.

٢٠ صُعْرَ ٱلْخُدُودِ كَأَنَّمَا   جُنِّحْنَ أَجْنِحَةَ ٱلنُّسُورِ

٢١ مُتَسَرْبِلَاتٍ بِٱلظَّلَا   مِ عَلَى ٱلسُّهُولَةِ وَٱلْوُعُورِ

٢٢ حَتَّى وَصَلْنَ بِنَا إِلَى   رَبِّ ٱلْمَدَائِنِ وَٱلْقُصُورِ

٢٣ مَا زَالَ قَبْلَ فِطَامِهِ   فِى سِنِّ مُكْتَهِلٍ كَبِيرِ

٩ أبو تمّام

١ السيف اصْدَقُ أنباءً من الكُتُبِ   فى حَدّهِ الحدُّ بين الجِدّ واللَّعِبِ

٢ بِيضُ الصفائح لا سُودُ الصحائف فى   متونهنّ جلاء الشكّ والرِّيَبِ

٣ والعِلْمُ فى شُهُبِ الأرماح لامعةً   بين الخميسَيْن لا فى السبعة الشُّهُبِ

٤ أين الرواية بل أين النجوم وما   صاغوه من زُخْرُفٍ فيها ومن كَذِبِ

٥ تخرُّصاً وأحاديثاً ملفَّقةً   ليست بِنَبْعٍ إذا عُدَّتْ ولا غَرَبِ

٦ عجائباً زعموا الأيّامَ مُجْفِلةً   عنهنّ فى صَفَرِ الأصفار أو رَجَبِ

---

2. A brilliant verse. *Matn* signifies the broad side of a sword and also the text of a book, both dispellers of confusion as to the issue. Note the *jinās* (*mukhtalif*) between *ṣafā'iḥ* and *ṣaḥā'if*, and the *ṭibāq* between *bīḍ* and *sūd*.

3. The "seven luminaries" are the sun, the moon, Saturn, Jupiter, Mars, Venus and Mercury. Note the contrast between the two (five-fold) armies and the seven shiners.

5. The *nab'* is the *chadara tenax*, a mountain-tree from which bows and arrows were made. The *gharab* is the pliant water-willow. The meaning is that the stories of the astrologers were neither firm nor even weak, they had no substance whatsoever.

6. *Ajfala*, like *ajlā* (the variant reading *mujliyatan* is quoted by al-Tibrīzī), is used of clouds dispersing to reveal the sun, see Lane 434. The phrase "Ṣafar of Ṣafars" is compared with "king of kings", a form to emphasise the portentousness. Ṣafar was ill-omened because its name also connoted "hunger"; Rajab connoted "fear".

7 And they terrified the people (foreboding) a dark calamity, when the tailed western star appeared.

8 And they catalogued the upper constellations as between moving and unmoving,

9 Determining the matter according to them; whereas they (the signs) are heedless which of them revolves in a "sphere" and which on a "pole".

10 Had they made clear any matter before it occurred, they would not have concealed what befell the idols and the crosses

11 In a notable victory too sublime to be described by any ordered verse or scattered discourse,

12 A victory in honour of which the gates of heaven open and earth comes forth in her new garments.

13 O day of the Battle of 'Ammūriya, (our) hopes have returned from you overflowing with honey-sweet milk;

14 You have left the fortunes of the sons of Islam in the ascendant, and the polytheists and the abode of polytheism in decline.

15 They had a mother for whom, had they hoped she might be ransomed, they would have given as ransom every loving mother and father,

16 Comely of face withal, so fit of physique that she reduced Chosroes to impotence, and utterly repelled Abū Karib.

17 From the age of Alexander or (even) before that—the forelocks of the nights might have become white, yet she has not become white;

18 A virgin, deflowered not by the hand of any accident (of fortune), neither has the ambition of time's turns aspired to (possess) her;

---

7. "A tailed western star": a comet appearing in the western sky.

8. "Constellations": the signs of the Zodiac. Four (Aries, Cancer, Libra and Capricornus) were said to be "moving"; four (Taurus, Leo, Scorpio and Aquarius) were "fixed"; four (Gemini, Virgo, Sagittarius and Pisces) were of double character. When the astrologers "placed" an event as occurring in a "fixed" sign, they gave the go-ahead; if the ascendant was a "moving" sign, action was to be avoided.

10. Had the stars really foretold the future, they would have predicted the defeat of the Christians of Byzantium. Note the *ṭibāq* between *baiyanat* and *tukhfi*.

11. Note the *ṭibāq* between *naẓm* and *nathr*.

12. *Tafattaḥu* is by licence for *tatafattaḥu*, see Wright, I, 65 B. "The gates of

٧ وخوّفوا الناس من دهياءَ مُظْلِمَةٍ   إذا بدا الكوكبُ الغَرْبىُّ ذو الذَّنَب

٨ وصيّروا الأَبْرُجَ العُلْيا مُرَتَّبَةً   ما كان منقلبًا أو غير منقلب

٩ يقضون بالأمر عنها وهْى غافلة   ما دار فى فَلَكٍ منها وفى قُطُب

١٠ لو بيّنت قطّ أمراً قبل موقعه   لم تُخْفِ ما حلّ بالأوثان والصُّلُب

١١ فَتْحَ الفتوح تعالى أن يحيط به   نَظْمٌ من الشعر أو نَثْرٌ من الخُطَب

١٢ فَتْحٌ تَفَتَّحُ أبوابُ السماء له   وتبرز الأرض فى أثوابها القُشُب

١٣ يا يومَ وقعة عَمُّورِيَّةَ انصرفت   منك المُنَى حُفَّلاً معسولةَ الحَلَب

١٤ أبقيتَ جَدَّ بنى الإسلام فى صُعُدٍ   والمشركين ودار الشرك فى صبب

١٥ أُمٌّ لهم لو رجوا أن تُفْتَدَى جعلوا   فداءها كلَّ أمٍّ بَرَّةٍ وأب

١٦ وبَرْزَةُ الوجه قد أَعْيَتْ رياضتُها   كِسْرَى وصدّت صدوداً عن أبى كَرِب

١٧ من عهد اسكندرٍ أو قبل ذلك قد   شابت نواصى الليالى وهى لم تَشِب

١٨ بِكْرٌ فما افترعتها كفُّ حادثةٍ   ولا ترقَّتْ إليها هِمَّةُ النُّوَب

---

heaven open" in life-giving rain, so that "earth comes forth in her new garments" of fresh herbs and flowers.

13. The usual spelling is ʿAmmūriya (see Yāqūt, *Muʿjam al-buldān*, VI, 226), which would not scan. *Ḥuffal* is pl. of *ḥāfil*, "a she-camel whose udders are full".

14. Note the *ṭibāq* between *islām* and *shirk*, and between *ṣuʿud* and *ṣabab*.

15. "A mother": sc. Amorium. Note the *jinās* between the metaphorical and literal uses of *umm*.

16. Abū Karib was one of the Tubbaʿs of Yemen (he died *ca.* A.D. 420); he is said to have conquered Persia and become a Jew, see P. Hitti, *History of the Arabs*, 60.

17. In al-Tibrīzī this verse is transposed with the verse following.

19 Till, when God had churned the years for her as a miserly woman churns milk, she was the cream of (all) the generations.

20 Black disaster came upon them, confounded at her whose name was the great deliverer from disasters.

21 The omen presaged ill fortune for her on the day of Anqira, when she was abandoned desolate as to her courtyards and areas.

22 When she beheld her sister devastated yesterday, devastation proved for her more contagious than the mange.

23 How many a gallant knight (lies) between her walls, his locks crimson from the hot blood gushing,

24 Dyed in his own blood by the usage of sword and lance, not the usage of religion and Islam!

25 Commander of the Faithful, you left the stones and wooden beams there abject to the fire.

26 You left behind there the pitchblack night as it were noonday, driven forth in the midst of her by a dawn of flame,

27 So that it was as though the robes of darkness forsook their (habitual) hue, or as though the sun had never set—

28 A radiance of fire whilst the shadows brooded, and an obscurity of smoke amidst a pallid noon,

29 The sun rising from that (conflagration) after it had set, and the sun sinking from that (smoke) when it had not sunk.

30 Destiny revealed itself plainly to her as the clouds (disperse to) reveal (the sun), (disclosing) a day of fierce battle, a day (at once) pure and defiled thereby.

31 The sun rose not that day upon any one of them (the enemy) that was a bridegroom, nor set upon any (of the victors) that was a bachelor.

32 The thronged quarter of Maiya circled by Ghailān was not more lovely as to (its) hillocks than the devastated quarter of her,

---

19. For the idiom of the miserly woman, see Lane 2693.

20. Disaster is compared with a stumbling, purblind camel dazzled by the splendour of Amorium.

21. For *naḥsan* al-Tibrīzī reads *barḥan* "evil". Anqira (Ancyra, Ankara) was plundered by al-Mu'taṣim in 838, shortly before he took Amorium.

22. "More contagious than the mange": see Lane 1981. Note the *jinās* between *kharibat* and *l-kharābu*.

23. Partial *jinās* between *qānī* and *ānī*.

24. According to the Sunna of the Prophet it was proper for an ageing man to stain his white hairs with henna, but not with a black dye. In al-Tibrīzī the reading *wa-l-khaṭṭi* is changed to *wa-l-ḥinnā'*, i.e. "and the henna is of his own blood".

١٩ حتّى إذا مخض اللّه السنين لها — مَخْضَ البخيلة كانت زبدةَ الحقبِ

٢٠ أَتَتْهم الكربة السوداء سادرةً — منها وكان اسمها فرّاجة الكُرَب

٢١ جرى لها الفأل نَحْسًا يوم أَنْقِرَةٍ — إذ غودرت وحشةَ السّاحات والرُّحَب

٢٢ لمّا رأت أُختها بالأمس قد خربت — كان الخراب لها أعدى من الجَرَب

٢٣ كم بين حيطانها من فارسٍ بَطَلٍ — قانى الذوائب من آنى دمٍ سَرِب

٢٤ بسُنّة السيف والخطّيِّ من دمه — لا سُنّةِ الدين والإسلام مختضب

٢٥ لقد تركتَ أميرَ المؤمنين بها — للنار يومًا ذليل الصخر والخشب

٢٦ غادَرْتَ فيها بهيمَ الليل وهو ضُحىً — يشلّه وَسْطَها صبحٌ من اللهب

٢٧ حتّى كأنّ جلابيب الدجى رغبت — عن لونها وكأنّ الشمس لم تغب

٢٨ ضوءٌ من النار والظلماءُ عاكفةٌ — وظلمة من دخانٍ فى ضُحىً شَحِب

٢٩ فالشمس طالعةٌ من ذا وقد أفلت — والشمس واجبة من ذا ولم تجب

٣٠ تَصَرَّحَ الدهرُ تصريح الغمام لها — عن يوم هيجاءَ منها طاهرٍ جُنُب

٣١ لم تطلع الشمس منهم يومَ ذاك على — بانٍ بأهل ولم تغرب على عَزَب

٣٢ ما رَبْعُ مَيَّةَ معمورًا يطيف به — غيلان أَبْهَى رُبًى من ربعها الخَرِب

---

26. Note the *ṭibāq* between *l-laili*, *ḍuḥan* and *ṣubḥun*.

28. This verse displays a perfect combination of *muqābala* and *ṭibāq*.

29. Again *muqābala* and *ṭibāq*.

30. "Pure" because the slain were justly put to the sword; "defiled" because the captive women were outraged.

31. The menfolk of the defenders were all slain, whilst the victors enjoyed the pleasures of the widows and daughters. For the idiom *bānin bi-ahlin* see Lane 261. For *minhum* al-Tibrīzī prefers the reading *fīhi*. Note the double *ṭibāq*.

32. Maiya was the beloved of the poet Ghailān (Dhu 'l-Rumma). Note the complex *jinās* and *ṭibāq*.

33 Neither were the cheeks (of lovely maidens) suffused with blood out of shyness more delectable to the beholder than her dust-stained cheek—

34 An ugliness by which our eyes are sufficed, so that they do not crave for any sort of visible beauty or marvellous sight,

35 And a lovely dénouement of visible consequences whose cheerfulness resulted from an evil dénouement.

36 Unbelief did not know for how many ages fate was lying in wait for it between the tawny (lances) and the bows—

37 The contriving of one who clung to God, who took revenge for God, whose whole desire was for God, who waited (on God),

38 (A huntsman) glutted by victory, unblunted ever his spearpoints, never debarred from (taking) the spirit of any well-protected (foeman),

39 Who never raided a people, who never rushed upon a land except there preceded him an army of terror.

40 Had he not led a massive troop on the day of battle, he would have been accompanied by a clamorous troop consisting of himself, alone.

41 God smote through you the twain towers of her and destroyed her—and had other than God smitten through you, you would not have hit the mark—

42 After they had entangled her about, confident in her; and God is the key to the gate of the (most) entangled citadel.

43 Their commander said, "(This is) no pasture at hand to the grazers, and the coming down (to this waterhole) is not from near"—

44 (Entertaining) hopes, but the points of swords and edges of ravishing lances despoiled them of the attainment of their whispering thought.

---

33. The variant *nāẓirī* for *nāẓirin* is recorded.

34. Note the *ṭibāq*.

35. The dénouement was "lovely" for the Muslims and "evil" for the Byzantines.

36. For *lam* al-Tibrīzī records *lau*, and for *l-manīyatu* the variant *l-ʿawāqibu*.

٣٣ ولا الخدودُ وقد أُدْمِينَ من خجلٍ　　أشْهَى إلى ناظرٍ من خدّها التّرِب

٢٤ سَمَاجَةٌ غَنِيَتْ منّا العيونُ بها　　عن كلّ حسن بدا أو منظرٍ عَجَب

٢٥ وحُسْنُ مُنْقَلَبٍ تبدو عواقبُه　　جاءت بشاشتُه من سوء منقلب

٣٦ لم يعلم الكفرُ كم من أعْصُرٍ كمنت　　له المنيّة بين السُّمر والقُضُب

٣٧ تدبيرُ معتصمٍ باللّه منتقمٍ　　للّه مرتغبٍ فى اللّه مرتقب

٣٨ ومُطْعَمِ النصر لم تَكْهَم أسنّتُه　　يومًا ولا حُجِبَت عن روح محتجِب

٣٩ لم يَغْزُ قومًا ولم يَنْهَد إلى بلدٍ　　إلّا تقدّمه جيش من الرُّعُب

٤٠ لو لم يقد جحفلاً يوم الوغى لغدا　　من نفسه وَحْدَها فى جحفلٍ لَجِب

٤١ رمى بك اللّه بُرْجَيْها فهدّمها　　ولو رمى بك غير اللّه لم تُصِب

٤٢ من بعد ما أشّبوها واثقين بها　　واللّه مفتاح باب المعقل الأَشِب

٤٣ وقال ذو أمرهم لا مرتعٌ صَدَدٌ　　للسارحين وليس الوِرْد من كَثَب

٤٤ أمانيًا سلبتهم نُجْحَ هاجسها　　ظُبَى السيوف وأطراف القنا السُّلُب

37. The poet puns on the caliph's name. There is *ṭibāq* (*lāḥiq*) between *murtaghibin* and *murtaqibin*, whose order is reversed by al-Tibrīzī.

38. Note the *jinās* (*al-ishtiqāq*) between *ḥujibat* and *muḥtajibi*.

41. The idea of God smiting through the caliph is based on Koran, VIII, 17.

42. "Entangled": i.e. with defenders and defences.

44. "Ravishing": *sulub* (pl. of *salib*) may also mean "tall". Note the *jinās*.

45 Truly the twain deaths (proceeding) from white (swords) and tawny (lances) were the twain buckets of twain lives (procured by and procuring) water and herbage.

46 You replied to (the call of) a Zibaṭrian voice, for which you poured out the cup of slumber and the sweet saliva of loving maidens.

47 The heat of the frontiers set ablaze diverted you from the coolness of (their) teeth and their pebbly saliva.

48 You answered it (the voice), baring the sword unsheathed, and had you answered with other than the sword, no (true) answer would you have given,

49 So that you left the tentpole of polytheism uprooted, not turning aside to the pegs and ropes.

50 When Theophilus saw war with his own eyes—and the meaning of war is derived from spoliation—

51 He proceeded to (seek to) divert its flow by (the expending of great) moneys; but the surging and fluctuating sea overpowered him.

52 Ah, the sedate earth was violently shaken by it (the army), by reason of an expedition to call (the offender) to account, not an expedition to procure gain.

53 He (the caliph) did not expend gold exceeding in multitude the pebbles, being in need of gold;

54 Surely the lions, the lions of the thicket—their ambition on the day of horrid (battle) is fixed on the plundered, not upon plunder.

55 He (Theophilus) turned his back, the lance having bridled his speech in a silence, below which (his) bowels were in (great) clamour.

56 He gave over his nearest associates to avert disaster, and departed, urging on the fleetest of his riding-beasts in flight,

---

45. The swords and lances brought death to the enemy and life-giving provisions (see line 43) to the Muslims. Note the *muqābala* and compound *ṭibāq*.

46. When Zibaṭra (a town lying on the frontiers of Byzantium) was taken by the Byzantines, a Muslim woman, laid hands upon by the Christians who would carry her into captivity, called out "*Wā-Mu'taṣimā!*". Report of this was brought to the caliph as he held in his hand a cup of wine; he laid it aside and ordered mobilisation and the attack on Amorium. The caliph forewent the pleasures of the marriage-bed (*'urub* is pl. of *'arūb*, "a woman passionately loving her husband") and of sleep to answer the appeal of the Zibaṭrian woman.

٤٥ إنّ الحِمامَيْن من بِيضٍ ومن سُمُرٍ   دَلْوَا الحياتَيْن من ماءٍ ومن عُشُبِ

٤٦ لبّيتَ صوتاً زِبَطْرِيّاً هرقتَ له   كأس الكرى ورُضابَ الخُرَّد العُرُبِ

٤٧ عداكَ حَرُّ الثغور المستضامة عن   برد الثغور وعن سلسالها الحَصِبِ

٤٨ أجبتَهُ معلنًا بالسيف منصلتًا   ولو أجبتَ بغير السيف لم تُجِبِ

٤٩ حتّى تركتَ عمودَ الشرك منقعرًا   ولم تعرّج على الأوتاد والطُّنُبِ

٥٠ لمّا رأى الحرب رأيَ العين تُوفَلِسٌ   والحرب مشتقّة المعنى من الحَرَبِ

٥١ غدا يصرّف بالأموال جَرْيَتَها   فعزَّه البحرُ ذو التيّار والحَدَبِ

٥٢ هيهات زُعْزِعت الأرضُ الوَقُور به   عن غَزْوِ محتسب لا غزوِ مكتسب

٥٣ لم ينفق الذهب المربى بكثرته   على الحصى وبه فقرٌ الى الذهب

٥٤ إنّ الأُسُودَ أُسُودَ الغاب همّتها   يوم الكريهة في المسلوب لا السَّلَبِ

٥٥ وَلّى وقد ألجم الخطّى منطقه   بسكتةٍ تحتها الأحشاء في صَخَبِ

٥٦ أَحْذَى قرابينه صرف الردى ومضى   يحتثّ أَنْجَى مطاياه من الهرب

50. Theophilus reigned 829–42, see Hitti 301. "From spoliation": one of the meanings assigned to *ḥarab*, see Lane 540; the word also means "grief". Note the *jinās* (*al-mushābih*).

51. By "sea" the poet refers to the army attacking in *waves*.

53. The campaign was not undertaken for loot but for revenge.

55. In his commentary on this verse al-Ṣūlī observed that the "clamour" of the enemy's "bowels" was a reference to the trepidation of his heart, not to be taken literally in the physical sense of breaking wind.

57 Put in charge of the high land to overlook, speeded by fear, not by joy!

58 If he ran from the heat of it (the raging battle) as an ostrich runs, yet you had made broad its furnace with the abundance of faggots—

59 Ninety thousand men like lions of (the mountain) al-Sharā, whose skins were ripened before the ripening of the figs and the grapes.

60 Ah, many a (Muslim) soul there was that rejoiced, when the last of them was plucked up; and had it been drenched in musk, it would not have been (so) redolent (with joy).

61 And (there was) many a one enraged, whom the white swords brought back from their destruction live with satisfaction, dead as to rage.

62 War raged in a narrow strait, where the warriors crouch humbly upon their knees.

63 How many a radiant moon was captured under the radiance of it (the battle), how many a gleaming molar under the cloud of it!

64 How many a means there was of coming to the curtained virgin, through cutting the cords of the necks (of their menfolk)!

65 How many a slender branch shaking on a sandhill the quivering drawn blades of the Indian (swords) attained!

66 White (blades)—when they were drawn from their sheaths, they returned with better right to the (Byzantine women) white of body than their veils.

67 Caliph of Allah, may Allah reward your strivings on behalf of the roots of the faith and Islam and honour!

68 You have beheld the greater repose, and you have perceived that it is not attained save over a bridge of toil.

69 Were there any joined tie of kinship between the vicissitudes of time, or any intact right to respect,

---

57. "To overlook": to spy out the land and see the best road of escape.

59. For al-Sharā, see Lane 1545. "Whose skins were ripened": i.e. for the plucking hand of death.

60. Note the *double entendre* on the alternative meanings of *ṭāba*.

61. Note the double *ṭibāq*.

62. For *al-kumātu* al-Tibrīzī reads *al-qiyāmu*, but comments on the variant. "Humbly": i.e. weighed down by their heavy accoutrement.

63. Note the double *jinās*. The reference is to the captive women.

٥٧ موكَّلا بيفاع الأرض يُشرفه   من خفّة الخوف لا من خفّة الطرب

٥٨ إن يَعْدُ من حرّها عَدْوَ الظليم فقد   أوسعتَ جاحمها من كثرة الحطب

٥٩ تسعون ألفًا كآسادِ الشرى نَضِجَتْ   جلودُهم قبل نضج التين والعنب

٦٠ يا رُبَّ حَوْباءَ لمّا اجتُثّ دابرُهم   طابت ولو ضُمّخت بالمسك لم تطب

٦١ ومُغْضَبٍ رجعت بِيضُ السيوف به   حيَّ الرضا من رداهم ميّت الغضب

٦٢ والحرب قائمة فى مأزقٍ لَجِجٍ   تجثو الكماة به صُغْرًا على الركب

٦٣ كم نِيلَ تحت سناها من سنا قمرٍ   وتحت عارضها من عارضٍ شَنِبِ

٦٤ كم كان فى قطع أسباب الرقاب بها   الى المخدّرة العذراء من سبب

٦٥ كم أحرزتْ قُضُبُ الهندىّ مصلتةً   تهتزّ من قُضُبٍ تهتزّ فى كُثُب

٦٦ بيضٌ اذا انْتُضِيَتْ من حُجْبِها رجعت   أَحَقَّ بالبيض أبدانًا من الحُجُب

٦٧ خليفةَ اللّه جازى اللّه سعيك عن   جرثومة الدين والإسلام والحسب

٦٨ بَصُرْتَ بالراحة الكبرى فلم ترها   تُنال الّا على جِسْرٍ من التعب

٦٩ إن كان بين صروف الدهر من رَحِمٍ   موصولةٍ أو ذمامٍ غير منقضب

---

64. Note the *jinās*. "The curtained virgin": either the captive women, or Amorium which had not been conquered before.

65. Note the *jinās*. The "slender branch shaking on a sandhill" is a conventional description of a slim torso surmounting plump thighs.

66. Note the double *jinās*. For *abdānan* al-Tibrīzī reads *atrāban*. The swords earned the victors the right to unveil the women of the vanquished.

68. As of the repose of Paradise, attained after crossing the narrow bridge dividing Heaven from Hell.

70 Then there would exist the closest relationship between your victory-crowned days and the days of Badr.

71 They (the days of victory) have left the sons of sickly al-Aṣfar pale of face as their name, and brightened the faces of the Arabs.

10 IBN AL-RŪMĪ

1 Sweet sleep has been barred from my eyes by their preoccupation with copious tears.

2 What sleep (is possible) after the great misfortunes that have befallen Basra?

3 What sleep (is possible) after the Zanj have violated openly the sacred places of Islam?

4 This indeed is such an affair as could scarcely have arisen in the imagination.

5 Wide awake we have witnessed matters which it would have sufficed us were they visions seen in a dream.

6 The accursed traitor ventured how recklessly against her (Basra) and against God

7 And named himself without right an Imam—may God not guide aright his labours as Imam!

8 My soul cries alas for thee, O Basra, with a sigh like the blaze of a conflagration;

9 My soul cries alas for thee, O mine of excellences, with a sigh that makes me to bite my thumb;

---

70. "The days of Badr": the celebrated victory of A.D. 624, in which 300 Muslims led by the Prophet defeated a much larger force of the Meccans.

71. "The sons of the sickly al-Aṣfar": the Byzantines, traced by Arab genealogists to an ancestor named al-Aṣfar ("the Pale").

10 Sources: *Dīwān* (Cairo, n.d.), 419–27.
Khaldūn al-Kinānī, *Nuṣūṣ*, 29–30 (selected verses).

Metre: *khafīf*.

This poem commemorates one of the bloodiest incidents of the "Servile War", the long rebellion of the Zanj slaves, negroes from East Africa pressed into servitude in the saltpetre pans of lower Iraq. The insurrection lasted from A.D. 870 to 883; Basra was devastated in 257/871.

1. The poem opens with the suggestion of a *nasīb*, the theme being the stock sleeplessness of the distraught lover. *Al-sijāmi* is "an infinitive noun used as an epithet" (Lane 1312).

٧٠ فبين أيّامك اللاتى نُصِرْتَ بها   وبين أيّام بَدْرٍ أَقْرَبُ النسب

٧١ أَبْقَتْ بنى الأصفر المِمْراض كاسمهم   صُفْرَ الوجوه وجلّتْ أَوْجُهَ العرب

١٠ ابن الرومى

١ ذاد عن مقلتى لذيذَ المنام   شغلُها عنه بالدموع السجام

٢ أىّ نوم من بعد ما حلّ بالبـ   صرة ما حلّ من هناتٍ عظام

٣ أىّ نوم من بعد ما انتهك الزنـ   جُ جهارًا محارمَ الإسلام

٤ إنّ هذا من الأمور لأمرٌ   كاد أن لا يقوم فى الأوهام

٥ لرأينا مستيقظين أمورًا   حَسْبُنا أن تكون رؤيا منام

٦ أقدم الخائن اللعين عليها   وعلى اللّه أيّما إقدام

٧ وتسمّى بغير حقّ إمامًا   لا هدى اللّه سعيه من إمام

٨ لهف نفسى عليك أيّتها البصـ   رة لهفًا كمثل لهب الضرام

٩ لهف نفسى عليك يا معدن الخيـ   رات لهفًا يُعضّنى إبهامى

---

2. "Great misfortunes": lit. "serious things" (*hanāt* pl. of *hana*, see Wright, I, 278 B).

5. Note the *jinās* (*al-ishtiqāq*) between *ra'ainā* and *ru'yā*, and the *ṭibāq* between *mustaiqiẓīna* and *manāmi*.

6. "The accursed traitor": the 'Alid pretender calling himself 'Alī ibn Muḥammad ibn Aḥmad and nicknamed al-Burqu'ī ("the Veiled") who put himself at the head of the Zanj revolutionaries and declared that he was the Mahdi; he was ultimately killed in 270/883. For the construction with *aiyamā*, see Wright, II, 316 D, 317 A.

7. For *lā* + perfect signifying imprecation, see Wright, II, 304 C.

8. *Lahfa nafsī* is abbreviated for *yā lahfa nafsī*, cf. Wright, II, 87 A and see Lane 761. Note the *jinās* (*muḍāri'* or *lāḥiq*) between *lahfa* and *lahba*, and the *mubālagha* customary in comparing the sigh of the sorrowful with the flaming of a conflagration.

10 My soul cries alas for thee, O tabernacle of Islam, with a sigh whence my anguish is prolonged;

11 My soul cries alas for thee, O anchorage of the lands, with a sigh that shall continue for long years;

12 My soul cries alas for thy concourse that has perished; my soul cries alas for thy grievously injured glory.

13 Even whilst her inhabitants were enjoying the fairest circumstances, their slaves assailed them with (sudden) destruction.

14 They entered her as though they were portions of night when it has become shrouded in darkness.

15 What terror they (the inhabitants) beheld by reason of them (the Zanj)! What terror, fit to turn hoary the head of youth!

16 When they assailed them with their fire from right and left, from behind them and before,

17 How many a toper they choked with an (unexpected) draught! How many a feaster they choked with an (unpalatable) dish!

18 How many a man niggardly with his soul sought a way of escape, and they met his brow with the sword!

19 How many a brother beheld his brother felled to the ground, dusty of cheek, amongst (many) nobles (so) fallen!

20 How many a father beheld the dearest of his sons hoisted aloft on a trenchant blade!

21 How many a one most precious to his kinsmen they betrayed, since there was not one there to protect him!

22 How many a suckling child they weaned with the edge of the sword before the time of weaning!

23 How many a young virgin with the seal of God (upon her) they violated openly without any concealment!

24 How many a chaste maiden they carried into captivity, her face displayed without a veil!

---

11. Basra was of course the principal seaport of the Islamic Empire, as well as being at its zenith a leading religious and intellectual centre.

14. "Portions of night": a double reference to the stealth of the attack and the black skins of the Zanj attackers.

15. The particle *an* is to be supplied before *yashība*.

17. *Jinās* between *shāribin* and *sharābi*, *ṭā'imin* and *ṭa'āmi*.

18. It is to be noted that *jabīn* ("brow") also signifies "coward".

19. The *Dīwān* reading *turriba*(?) is clearly inferior to *tariba*.

١٠ لهف نفسى عليك يا قبّة الإسـ ـلام لهفًا يطول منه غرامى

١١ لهف نفسى عليك يا فُرضة البلـ ـدان لهفًا يبقى على الأعوام

١٢ لهف نفسى لجمعك المتفانى لهف نفسى لعزّك المستضام

١٣ بينما أهلها بأحسن حال إذ رماهم عبيدهم باصطلام

١٤ دخلوها كأنّهم قِطَعُ اللـيـ ـل إذا راح مدلهمّ الظلام

١٥ أىّ هول رأوا بهم أىّ هول حقّ منه يشيب رأس الغلام

١٦ إذ رموهم بنارهم من يمين وشمال وخلفهم وأمام

١٧ كم أغصّوا من شارب بشراب كم أغصّوا من طاعم بطعام

١٨ كم ضنين بنفسه رام منجى فتلقّوا جبينه بالحسام

١٩ كم أخ قد رأى أخاه صريعًا تَرِبَ الخدِّ بين صرعى كرام

٢٠ كم أب قد رأى عزيز بنيه وهو يُعْلَى بصارم صمصام

٢١ كم مفدّى فى أهله أسلموه حين لم يحمِه هنالك حامى

٢٢ كم رضيع هناك قد فطموه بشبا السيف قبل حين الفطام

٢٣ كم فتاة بخاتم اللّه بكرٍ فضحوها جهرًا بغير اكتتام

٢٤ كم فتاة مصونة قد سبوها بارزًا وجهها بغير لثام

---

21. "Most precious": lit. "deemed worthy of ransoming with one's own life". "They betrayed": perhaps rather, "they delivered over (to death)".

22. For *shabā*, *Nuṣūṣ* reads *shafā* with the same meaning.

23. For "the seal of God" as denoting virginity, see Lane 703, col. 1. For *iktitāmi* the reading *iḥtishāmi* ("respect") is given in *Nuṣūṣ*. Note the *ṭibāq* between *jahran* and *iktitāmi*.

24. For the *tamyīz* construction see Wright, II, 128 D.

25 They came upon them in the morning, and the people endured their cruelty through the length of a day that was as if a thousand years.

26 Who beheld them (the women) captives driven (like beasts), bleeding from head to foot?

27 Who beheld them in the partitioning between the Zanj, being divided amongst them by lots?

28 Who beheld them being taken as bondswomen, after themselves possessing bondswomen and servants?

29 I never recall what was perpetrated by the Zanj without it kindles what a conflagration in my heart;

30 I never recall what was perpetrated by the Zanj without I am anguished by the bitterness of humiliation.

31 Many a purchase they there cheapened that had long been very dear to the chafferers.

32 Many a house they there destroyed that was a shelter for the infirm and for orphans;

33 Many a palace they there broke into that had hitherto been difficult indeed of access.

34 Many a one there possessed of wealth and plenty they left in league with utter deprivation.

35 Many a people who passed the night in closest unity, they left their unity utterly disordered.

36 Turn aside, my two comrades, at Basra the brilliant, as one wasted with sickness turns aside,

37 And enquire of her—but answer is not to be found in her to any question, and who is there to speak for her?—

38 "Where is the clamour of them that dwelt in her? Where are her jostling markets?

39 Where is any ship sailing from her or sailing to her—ships raised up in the sea like landmarks?

40 Where are those palaces and mansions that were in her? Where is that well-secured edifice?"

---

27. The sharing up of the women is pictured as carried out after the Jāhilī usage of shuffling arrows for the partition of a carcase.

31. *Ṭibāq* between *arkhaṣūhā* and *ghalā*.

36. The poet now irregularly introduces the (usually opening) scene of addressing his two companions and calling upon them to halt awhile from the journey. The

٢٥ صبّحوهم فكابد القوم منهم   طولَ يوم كأنّه ألف عام
٢٦ من رآهنّ فى المساق سبايا   داميات الوجوه للأقدام
٢٧ من رآهنّ فى المقاسم وسطَ الزّ   نج يُقَسَّمْنَ بينهم بالسهام
٢٨ من رآهنّ يُتّخذن إماءً   بعد ملك الإماء والخدّام
٢٩ ما تذكّرتُ ما أتى الزنج إلّا   أضرم القلب أيّما إضرام
٣٠ ما تذكّرت ما أتى الزنج إلّا   أوجعتنى مرارةُ الإرغام
٣١ ربّ بيع هناك قد أرخصوه   طال ما قد غلا على السوّام
٣٢ ربّ بيت هناك قد أخربوه   كان مأوى الضعاف والأيتام
٣٣ ربّ قصر هناك قد دخلوه   كان من قبل ذاك صعب المرام
٣٤ ربّ ذى نعمة هناك ومالٍ   تركوه محالف الإعدام
٣٥ ربّ قوم باتوا بأجْمَع شمل   تركوا شملهم بغير نظام
٣٦ عَرِّجا صاحبيّ بالبصرة الزه   راء تعريجَ مدنفٍ ذى سقام
٣٧ فاسألوها ولا جوابَ لديها   لسؤالٍ ومن لها بالكلام
٣٨ أين ضوضاء ذلك الخلق فيها   أين أسواقها ذوات الزحام
٣٩ أين فُلك منها وفلك إليها   منشئات فى البحر كالأعلام
٤٠ أين تلك القصور والدور فيها   أين ذاك البنيان ذو الإحكام

---

description "as one wasted with sickness" links up with the first line of the poem, being a further stock attribution of the distraught lover.

39. I have emended *fīhā* to *minhā*. The second half of this couplet is a quotation (the figure is called *taḍmīn*) from Koran, LV, 24.

41 Those palaces have been changed into rubbish-mounds of ashes and heaped dust;

42 Flood and fire have been given authority over them, and their columns have crumbled down in utter destruction,

43 They have become empty of those that dwelt in them, and they are desolate; the eye descries nothing amongst those mounds

44 But hands and feet parted (from their bodies), flung aside amidst them skulls split asunder

45 And faces smeared with blood—may my father be a ransom for those bloody faces!—

46 Trampled down perforce in contempt and humiliation, after they were so long magnified and revered.

47 So you may see them, the winds blowing upon them, scattering over them as they pass dark dust,

48 Lowly and humbled, as if they were weeping, displaying their teeth—but not in a smile!

49 Rather, (my comrades), repair to the congregational mosque, if you be men apt to tarry,

50 And enquire of it—but answer is not to be found in it—"Where are its worshippers, who stood long in prayer?

51 Where are its throngers who used to throng it, passing all their time in recitation and fasting?

52 Where are its young men with their handsome faces? Where are its old men prudent and wise?"

53 What a calamity, what a mighty disaster has overtaken us, in (the loss of) those kinsmen!

54 How many we forsook—earnest ascetic, erudite scholar learned in his religion.

55 Ah, how I regret that I deserted them; but little avails my regret for their loss.

56 Ah, how I shall be shamed before them, when we meet together before the Judge of Judges!

57 What excuse shall we have to offer, what response to give, when we are summoned over the heads of mankind?

---

45. *Jinās* between *dimā'un* and *ad-dawāmī*. For the construction with *bi-abī*, see Wright, II, 162A.

46. Double *ṭibāq*.

٤١ بُدِّلَتْ تلكم القصور تلالاً   من رمادٍ ومن ترابٍ رُكام

٤٢ سُلِّط البثقُ والحريق عليها   فتداعت أركانها بانهدام

٤٣ وخَلَتْ من حلولها فهى قفرٌ   لا ترى العين بين تلك الإكام

٤٤ غير أيدٍ وأرجلٍ بائنات   نُبذت بينهنّ افلاق هام

٤٥ ووجوهٍ قد رمّلتها دماء   بأبى تلكم الوجوه الدوامى

٤٦ وُطِئَتْ بالهوان والذلّ قسرًا   بعد طول التبجيل والإعظام

٤٧ فتراها تسفى الرياح عليها   جاريات بهبوة وقتام

٤٨ خاشعات كأنّها باكيات   باديات الثغور لا لابتسام

٤٩ بل ألِمّا بساحة المسجد الجا   مع إن كنتما ذوى إلمام

٥٠ فاسألوه ولا جواب لديه   أين عبّاده الطوال القيام

٥١ أين عمّاره الأُلى عمّروه   دهرَهم فى تلاوة وصيام

٥٢ أين فتيانه الحسان وجوهًا   أين أشياخه أولو الأحلام

٥٣ أىّ خطب وأىّ رزء جليل   نالنا فى أولئك الأعمام

٥٤ كم خذلنا من ناسك ذى اجتهاد   وفقيه فى دينه علّام

٥٥ وا ندامى على التخلّف عنهم   وقليل عنهم غناء ندامى

٥٦ وا حيائى منهم اذا ما التقينا   وهمُ عند حاكم الحكّام

٥٧ أىّ عذر لنا وأىّ جواب   حين نُدْعَى على رؤوس الأنام

---

48. A grim touch of humour!
52. *Ṭibāq* between *fityān* and *ashyākh*.

58 "O My servants, were you not angry on My behalf, on behalf of Me, the Majestic, the Splendid?

59 Did you forsake your brethren and desert them—out upon you!—as ignoble men desert (their fellows)?

60 How did you not have compassion for (your) sisters (tied) in the ropes of slaves of the sons of Ham!

61 You were not jealous on account of My jealousy, so you abandoned My inviolable ones to those who defiled My sanctuary.

62 Surely he who was not jealous for My inviolable ones is no fit mate for chaste dwellers in the (heavenly) tents;

63 How should houri approve of a man's action, when he did not stand defender over the inviolable?"

64 Ah, how I shall be shamed before the Prophet, when he reproaches me concerning them with severest rebuke,

65 And I am all alone, when they rise up to accuse me, and the Prophet himself takes charge of the case against me on their behalf.

66 Picture how he will say to you, O men, when he reproaches you along with the reproachers,

67 "My community! Where were you, when there called upon you a free woman, of the noble women of the people?

68 'O Muhammad!' she shrieked, and why did there not rise up on her behalf the guardians of my right in my stead?

69 I did not answer her, for I was dead; but why was there not one man living to answer on behalf of my bones?"

70 May my father be a ransom for those bones, great men that they were! And may heaven water them with flood-charged clouds!

71 And upon them be blessing from the Sovereign (God) and peace fortified with peace!

72 Go forth, you nobles, light and heavy, against the vile slaves;

73 They managed well their enterprise whilst you were sleeping—shame, shame upon the sleep of the sleepers!

---

58. *Taḍmīn* of Koran, LV, 78.

61. *Ṭibāq* between *aḥalla* and *ḥarāmī*.

62. They do not qualify for the assignment of houris "restraining their glances" as described in Koran, LV, 56.

64. Note the *jinās*.

65. *Jinās* again.

٥٨ يا عبادى أما غضبتم لوجهى ذى الجلال العظيم والإكرام

٥٩ أخذلتم إخوانكم وقعدتم عنهمُ ويحكم قعودَ اللئام

٦٠ كيف لم تعطفوا على أخوات فى حبال العبيد من آل حام

٦١ لم تغاروا لغيرتى فتركتم حُرُماتى لمن أحلّ حرامى

٦٢ إنّ من لم يَغَرْ على حرماتى غير كفءٍ لقاصرات الخيام

٦٣ كيف ترضى الحوراء بالمرء فعلاً وهو من دون حرمةٍ لا يحامى

٦٤ وا حيائى من النبىّ اذا ما لامنى فيهمُ أشدّ الملام

٦٥ وانقطاعى اذا همُ خاصمونى وتولّى النبىّ عنهم خِصامى

٦٦ مثِّلوا قوله لكم أيّها النا س إذا لامكم مع اللوّام

٦٧ أُمّتى اين كنتمُ اذ دَعَتْنى حُرّةٌ من كرائم الأقوام

٦٨ صرخت يا محمداه فهلّا قام فيها رُعاة حقّى مقامى

٦٩ لم أُجِبْها اذ كنتُ ميتاً فلولا كان حىٌّ أجابها عن عظامى

٧٠ بأبى تلكم العظام عظاماً وسقتها السماء صوب الغمام

٧١ وعليها من المليك صلاة وسلام مؤكّد بسلام

٧٢ إنفروا أيها الكرام خفافًا وثقالاً الى العبيد الطغام

٧٣ أبرَموا أمرهم وأنتم نيام سوءةً سوءةً لنوم النيام

---

66. Once more *jinās*.
68. For the exclamatory form, see Wright, II, 94B.
69. *Ṭibāq* between *maitan* and *ḥaiyun*.
70. Note the *jinās* between the two meanings of *ʿiẓām*.
72. *Taḍmīn* of Koran, IX, 41.
73. Note the *jinās*.

74 Make true the belief of (your) brothers who had (high) expectations of you, and put their hopes in you (to help them) in all vicissitudes.

75 Exact vengeance for them, for that will be (grateful) to them as the restoring of their spirits to their bodies.

76 You did not comfort them by coming to their assistance, so do you now comfort them by taking revenge.

77 Deliver them that are captives: little (enough) is that by way of protection and observance of obligations.

78 The shame they suffered attaches to you, O men, because the ties of religion are as the ties of kinship.

79 If (now) you neglect (to punish) the accursed one, you will all be partners of the accursed one in his crimes.

80 Hasten against him with resolution before deliberation, and with bridling before saddling;

81 He who has put his saddle on the back of a generous steed, prohibited to him (thereafter) is the binding of the girth.

82 Do not tarry long away from eternal Paradise, for you are not in an abode of tarrying;

83 So purchase the abiding things with (the price of) the meanest (mundane) goods, and sell detachment from them for eternal life.

11 AL-BUḤTURĪ

1 I have guarded my soul from that which would defile my soul, and I have exalted myself above the pittance of every poltroon,

2 And I held firm when fortune shook me violently, seeking to contrive my fall and overthrow.

3 Bare sufficiency of the dregs of livelihood (remains) to me, which the days doled out in short measure, a doling out of defrauding.

---

81. *Jinās* again.
82. *Jinās* again.
83. Note the *ṭibāq*.

11 Sources: *Dīwān* (Constantinople, 1300/1883), 108–110.
Dīwān (Beirut, 1381/1962), I, 190–4.
Muntakhab, II, 275–80.
Nuṣūṣ, 15–17.

٧٤ صدّقوا ظنّ إخوة أملوكم ورجوكم لنوبة الأيّام

٧٥ أدرِكوا ثأرهم فذاك لديهم مثل ردّ الأرواح فى الأجسام

٧٦ لم تُقرّوا العيون منهم بنصرٍ فأقرّوا عيونهم بانتقام

٧٧ أنقِذوا سبيهم وقلّ لهم ذا ك حفاظاً ورعيةً للذمام

٧٨ عارهم لازمْ لكم أيّها النا س لأنّ الأديان كالأرحام

٨٩ إن قعدتم عن اللعين فانتم شركاء اللعين فى الآثام

٨٠ بادروه قبل الرويّة بالعز م وقبل الإسراج بالإلجام

٨١ من غدا سرجه على ظهر طرف فحرام عليه شدّ الحزام

٨٢ لا تطيلوا المقام عن جنّة الخلـ د فأنتم فى غير دار مقام

٨٣ فٱشتروا الباقيات بالعَرَض الأد نى وبيعوا انقطاعه بالدوام

١١ البحترى

١ صُنْتُ نفسى عمّا يُدنّس نفسى وترفّعتُ عن جَدا كلّ جِبْس

٢ وتماسكتُ حيث زعزعنى الدهـ رُ ٱلتماساً منه لتعسى ونُكْسى

٣ بُلَغٌ من صُبابة العيش عندى طفّفتْها الأيّامُ تَطْفيفَ بَخْس

Metre: *khafīf*.

1. "Pittance": for *jadā* meaning "donation", see Lane 393, col. 2.

2. For *ḥaithu* the reading *ḥīna* is given in the Constantinople edition and in *Muntakhab*.

3. For *bakhs*, cf. Koran, XII, 20.

4 Far is the difference between him who comes down every day to drink whose draught is uninterrupted, and him who comes down to drink after three days' thirsting.

5 It is as though time's favours have come to be directed (only) towards the ignoblest of the ignoble;

6 And my purchasing of Iraq was a course of folly, after my selling Syria in a sale of utter loss.

7 So do not go on testing me (now), to prove me in this (present) misfortune, and then to dislike the feel of me;

8 For of old you have known me for a man of certain qualities, disdainful of base things, refractory.

9 I have been disquieted by my cousin's harshness, (coming) after his (former) gentleness and cordiality,

10 And when I am wronged, I am apt to be seen not to pass the morning where I passed the previous night.

11 Anxieties attended my lodging, therefore I turned my sturdy she-camel in the direction of the white (palace) of Ctesiphon

12 Consoling myself for what chances had come (upon me), and grieving for a decayed abode of the House of Sāsān.

13 Successive vicissitudes reminded me of them—and vicissitudes are apt to make a man remember, and forget—

14 When they dwelt at ease in the shadow of a tall (palace) overlooking (the surrounding land), wearying and weakening the eyes (that gazed at it),

15 Its gate locked against the mountain of al-Qabq, as far as the broad lands of Khilāṭ and Muks—

16 Abodes that were not like the traces of the encampment of Suʿdā in smooth-swept wastes of wildernesses,

---

4. "After three days' thirsting": *khims* is used of a camel which drinks one day, then misses three days, then drinks again on the fifth day.

6. The poet regrets having left Syria to take up residence in Baghdad. Al-Buḥturī was born in Manbij, and after an early career in Maʿarrat al-Nuʿmān he joined Abū Tammām at the court of Malik b. Ṭauq, governor of Iraq. Thereafter in an eventful life he shuttled to and fro between Iraq and Syria; see *Encycl. of Isl.*[2], I, 1289–90. Note the *ṭibāq*.

9. "My cousin's harshness": the poet means the caliph al-Muntaṣir, who traced his descent from the Banū ʿAdnān, "cousins" of his own tribe the Banū Qaḥṭān. The context suggests that this famous poem was written after the death of al-Mutawakkil, in whose assassination al-Buḥturī is said to have been implicated.

12. "The white (palace) of Ctesiphon": "And al-Abyaḍ is also the palace of the

٤ وبعيدٌ ما بين وارد رِفْهٍ   عَلَلٍ شُرْبُه ووارد خِمْسِ

٥ وكأنّ الزمان أَصْبَحَ محمو   لًا هواه مع الأَخَسِّ الأَخَسِّ

٦ وٱشترائى العراق خُطَّةَ غَبْنٍ   بعد بيعى الشآم بيعةَ وَكْسِ

٧ لا تَرُزْنى مزاولًا لاختبارى   عند هذى البلوى فتُنْكِرَ مسّى

٨ وقديمًا عَهِدْتنى ذا هَنَاتٍ   آبياتٍ على الدنيئات شُمْسِ

٩ ولقد رابنى نُبُوُّ ابن عمّى   بعد لين من جانبَيْه وأُنْسِ

١٠ وإذا ما جُفِيتُ كنتُ حريًّا   أن أُرَى غير مُصْبِحٍ حيث أُمْسى

١١ حضرتْ رَحْلِىَ الهمومُ فوجّهـ   ـتُ إلى أبيض المدائن عَنْسى

١٢ أتسلّى عن الحظوظ وآسى   لمحلٍّ من آل ساسانَ دَرْسِ

١٣ ذكّرْتنيهم الخطوب التوالى   ولقد تُذْكِر الخطوب وتُنْسى

١٤ وهمُ خافضون فى ظلّ عالٍ   مُشْرِفٍ يُحْسِر العيونَ ويُخْسِى

١٥ مُغْلَقٍ بابُه على جبل القَبْـ   ـقِ إلى دارتَى خِلاطٍ ومُكْسِ

١٦ حِلَلٌ لم تكن كأطلال سُعْدَى   فى قِفَارٍ من البسابس مُلْسِ

Chosroes in al-Madā'in. It was one of the wonders of the world, and remained standing until the days of al-Muktafī in about the year 290. Then it was destroyed, and there was built on its parapets the foundation of al-Tāj in the caliph's dwelling (Baghdad)." Yāqūt, I, 100, where this passage from the poem is cited.

15. Qabq (or al-Qabq) was the name given to a mountain adjacent to Bāb al-Abwāb (the "Iron Gate", now Derbent, at the eastern end of the Caucasus), "originally fortified against invaders from the N. at some date not determined, traditionally by Anūshirwān" (*Encycl. of Isl.*², I, 835). Khilāṭ was a state in eastern Armenia with a capital city of the same name. Muks was a place also in Armenia.

16. The poet compares the ruins which he is about to describe with the deserted encampments so beloved of the Jāhilī poets. Su'dā is a common Bedouin woman's name, frequently mentioned in the old poems.

17 And (high) endeavours which, but for partiality on my part, the endeavour of 'Ans and 'Abs could not match.

18 Time has transformed their erstwhile (splendour) out of its (pristine) freshness, till they have now become worn-out rags of (cast-off) garments.

19 It is as though the Jirmāz, now that it is no longer thronged and is fallen into decay, is the edifice of a tomb;

20 Were you to see it, you would know that the nights have conducted a funeral in it, after a wedding-feast,

21 Whilst it informs you of the marvels of a people, the account of whom is not clouded by any obscurity.

22 When you behold the picture of Antioch, you are alarmed (as) between Byzantium and Persia,

23 The Fates there waiting, whilst Anūshirwān urges on the ranks under the royal banner

24 (Robed) in green over gold, proudly flaunting the dye of the (red) tumeric,

25 And the press of men before him, all silent, lowering their voices,

26 Some cautiously reaching out the foreshaft of a lance, some fearfully averting the spear-points with a shield.

27 The eye describes them as really alive, signalling like the dumb one to another;

28 My doubt concerning them augments, until my hands explore and touch them.

29 Abu 'l-Ghauth gave me to drink, not sparingly, over the two armies a hasty draught

30 Of a wine you would believe to be a night-irradiating star, or the rays of a sun,

---

17. "But for partiality on my part": i.e. as an Arab, towards the Arabs. 'Abs and 'Ans were the names of Arab tribes.

19. The Beirut edition reads *wa-ikhlāqihi* for *wa-ikhlālihi*. The Jirmāz was "a great building in al-Abyaḍ at Ctesiphon, now disappeared" (Yāqūt, III, 88).

21. Note the *ṭibāq*.

22. Antioch was besieged and destroyed by Anūshirwān in 540, during the perennial wars between Sasanian Persia and Byzantium.

23. *Dirafs* is the arabicised form of the Persian *dirafsh*.

24. The *wars* yielded a dye described alternatively as intensely red and intensely yellow, see Lane 2936–7.

١٧ وساعٍ لولا المحاباة منّى — لم تُطِقْها مسعاة عَنْسٍ وعَبْسِ

١٨ نقل الدهرُ عهدهنّ عن الجِدّ — ة حتّى غدَوْن أنْضاءَ لُبْسِ

١٩ فكأنّ الجِرْمازَ مِنْ عَدَمِ الأُنْ — سِ وإِخْلالِه بنيّةُ رَمْسِ

٢٠ لو تراه علمتَ أنّ الليالى — جعلت فيه مأتمًا بعد عُرْسِ

٢١ وهو يُنبيك عن عجائب قومٍ — لا يشابُ البيانُ فيه بلَبْسِ

٢٢ فاذا ما رأيتَ صورة أَنْطا — كِيَّةَ ارْتَعْتَ بين رومٍ وفُرْسِ

٢٣ والمنايا مَوَاثِلٌ وأنوشر — وان يُزْجِي الصفوف تحت الدِرَفْسِ

٢٤ فى ٱخضرارٍ من اللباس على أَصْ — فَرَ يختالُ فى صبيغة وَرْسِ

٢٥ وعِرَاكُ الرجال بين يديه — فى خُفُوتٍ منهم وإغماض جَرْسِ

٢٦ من مُشيحٍ يهوى بعامل رُمْحٍ — ومُليحٍ من السنان بتُرْسِ

٢٧ تَصِفُ العينُ أنّهم جِدُّ أحْيا — ءٍ لهم بينهم إشارة خُرْسِ

٢٨ يغتلى فيهمُ ٱرتيابىَ حتّى — تتقرّاهمُ يداى بلَمْسِ

٢٩ قد سقانى ولم يُصَرِّدْ أبو الغو — ث على العسكرين شربة خَلْسِ

٣٠ من مدام تقولها هى نَجْمٌ — أَضْوَأَ الليل أو مُجاجة شمسِ

---

26. *Muntakhab* reads *bi-ḥāmili* for *bi-ʿāmili*. Note the *malāʾama*, and the internal rhyme (and partial *jinās*) between *mushīḥin* and *mulīḥin*.

27. For this use of *jiddu* see Wright, II, 279C.

28. "My doubt": sc. as to whether they are animate or inanimate.

29. Abu 'l-Ghauth was the *kunya* of al-Buḥturī's son.

30. "The rays of a sun": *mujāja* ("spittle") is attributed to the sun in the same sense as *luʿāb*, "a thing that one sees, as though descending from the sky, at the time of the mid-day heat, resembling cobwebs" (Lane 2662, 2689).

31 And you behold it renewing with joy and delight the drinker as he sips,

32 Poured into the glass of every heart, and it the beloved of every soul.

33 And I imagined that Kisrā Abarwīz (himself) was handing me (the wine), and that al-Balahbadh was my boon-companion.

34 Was it a dream that covered my eyes, so that I wavered, or vain hopes transforming my thought and my conjecture?

35 And it was as though the great hall of marvellous workmanship were a spacious tract beside a rugged mountain,

36 It being deemed, because of the melancholy of its appearance to one visiting (it) in the morning or the evening,

37 (To be) a man disquieted on parting from the society of a beloved companion, or constrained to separate from a bride.

38 The (passage of the) nights has reversed its luck, and Jupiter has spent the night there as a star of ill omen.

39 Yet it displays fortitude, for all that there lies upon it the anchored breast of Fate.

40 It disgraces it not that it has been robbed of brocaded carpets and plundered of white silk curtains,

41 Soaring (as it is) with lofty battlements raised up on the heads of Raḍwā and Quds,

42 Apparelled in white, all that you see of them is waist-wrappers of cotton.

43 It is not known whether it is the work of men for jinn which they have taken to inhabit, or the work of jinn for men.

44 Yet I see it testifying that its royal builder was by no means failing in lavishness;

45 And it is as though I see the ranks of the people, when I reach the limit of my perception,

46 And as though the embassies were exposed to the sun there, weary of standing behind the throng, held back (to await their turn),

---

33. Kisrā Abarwīz: the arabicised form of Khusrau Parvīz, the son of Anūshirwān, acting as *sāqī* to his royal father in the same way as Abu 'l-Ghauth was to the poet.

36. For the irregular formation *yutaẓannā* from the root ẒNN, see Lane 1925.

38. Jupiter was normally regarded as auspicious.

٣١ وتراها اذا أجدّت سروراً وآرتياحًا للشارب المتحسّي

٣٢ أُفْرِغَتْ في الزجاج من كلّ قلب فهي محبوبةٌ إلى كلّ نفس

٣٣ وتوهّمتُ أن كِسْرَى أَبَرْوِيـ زَ معاطيَّ والبَلَهْبَذُ أُنْسي

٣٤ حُلُمٌ مُطْبِقٌ على الشكّ عيني أم أمانٍ غيّرن ظنّي وحدسي

٣٥ وكأنّ الإيوانَ من عجب الصنْـ عة جَوْبٌ في جنب أَرْعَنَ جِلْسِ

٣٦ يُتَظَنَّى من الكآبة أن يبْـ دو لعينَي مُصَبِّحٍ أو مُمَسِّي

٣٧ مُزْعَجًا بالفراق عن أُنْس إِلْفٍ عَزَّ أو مُرْهَقًا بتطليق عِرْس

٣٨ عكست حظّه الليالي وبات الـ مشتري فيه وهو كوكب نَحْس

٣٩ فهو يُبْدِي تجلُّدًا وعليه كلكلٌ من كلاكل الدهر مُرْسي

٤٠ لم يَعِبْهُ أن بُزَّ من بُسُط الديـ باج وٱستُلَّ من ستور الدِّمَقْسِ

٤١ مُشْمَخِرٌّ تعلو له شرفاتٌ رُفِعت في رؤوس رَضْوَى وقُدْس

٤٢ لابساتٌ من البياض فما تُبْـ صِرُ منها إلّا غلائلَ بُرْس

٤٣ ليس يُدْرَى أَصُنْعُ إِنْسٍ لِجِنٍّ سكنوه أم صنع جِنٍّ لإِنْس

٤٤ غير أنّي أراه يشهد أن لم يك بانيه في الملوك بِنِكْس

٤٥ فكأنّيَ أرى المراتب والقو م إذا ما بلغتُ آخر حِسّي

٤٦ وكأنّ الوفود ضاحين حَسْرَى من وقوفٍ خَلْفَ الزحام وخُنْس

---

41. Raḍwā is a mountain in the neighbourhood of Medina, Quds a mountain in Nejd.

42. For *ghalā'ila* the Constantinople text reads *falā'ila* "topknots". The reference is presumably to the gossamer hangings referred to in *v.* 30.

47 And as though the singing-girls, amid the pavilions, were swaying, as between brownness (of lips) and dark redness,

48 And as though the encounter were but two days since, and the hasty parting but yesterday,

49 And as though he who would follow after is eager to overtake them on the morning of the fifth day.

50 Thronged with joy for a time, then its quarters were given over to sorrow and mourning.

51 All I can do is to succour it with tears dedicated in mortmain to deep affection.

52 That I have, yet the house is not my house by virtue of any proximity to it, neither is the race my race

53 Other than the favour her people did to my people; they have planted the best of plantations of its fulness.

54 They strengthened our kingdom and confirmed its powers with heroic warriors clad in armour;

55 They gave succour against the squadrons of Aryāṭ with a thrust at the throats and a piercing,

56 And I see myself thereafter in love with noblemen altogether, of whatever stock and base.

12 IBN AL-MU'TAZZ

1 When the horizon burst forth with light like the smile of crimson lips

2 And the tresses of darkness were flecked with white, and the night star purposed to drowse,

3 We led forth against the wide-eyed wild cows and the antelopes a sagacious bitch, much feared in the encounter,

47. For *yarajjaḥna* (short for *yatarajjaḥna*) the Constantinople text gives the perhaps superior reading *yurajji'na* "trilling".

48. In this and the following verse the poet meditates on the familiar theme of the shortness of human destinies and the passing of dynasties.

50. Note the *ṭibāq*.

54. *Muntakhab* reads *bi-ḥumātin* for *bi-kumātin*.

55. Aryāṭ was the Abyssinian commander who led the invasion of South Arabia in the "Year of the Elephant"; see Nicholson, *Literary History of the Arabs*, pp. 27–8. Yemen was at that time a Persian protectorate.

56. *Muntakhab* reads *wa-jinsi* for *wa-issi*.

٤٧ وكأنّ القيان وسط المقاصيـ   ـر يرجّحن بين حُوّ ولُعْس

٤٨ وكأنّ اللقاء أوّل من أمْـ   ـس ووَشْكَ الفراق أوّل أمْس

٤٩ وكأنّ الذى يريد اتّباعاً   طامعٌ فى لحوقهم صُبْحَ خَمْس

٥٠ عمرت للسرور دهراً فصارت   للتعزّى رباعُهم والتأسّى

٥١ فلها أن أُعينها بدموعٍ   مُوقَفَاتٍ على الصبابة حُبْس

٥٢ ذاك عندى وليست الدارُ دارى   باقترابٍ منها ولا الجنس جِنسى

٥٣ غير نُعْمَى لأهلها عند أهلى   غرسوا من ذكائها خير غَرْس

٥٤ أيَّدوا ملكنا وشدّوا قواه   بكماةٍ تحت السنَوَّر حُمْس

٥٥ وأعانوا على كتائب أرْيَا   طَ بطَعْنٍ على النحور ودَعْس

٥٦ وأرانى من بعد أَكْلَفُ بالأشـ   ـراف طُرًّا من كلّ سِنْخٍ وإسّ

١٢ ابن المعتزّ

١ لمّا تفرّى الأُفْقُ بالضياء   مثل ابتسام الشَّفَة اللمياء

٢ وشَمِطَتْ ذوائبُ الظلماء   وهَمَّ نجمُ الليل بالإغفاء

٣ قُدْنا لعِينِ الوحش والظباء   داهيةً محذورةَ اللقاء

---

12 Sources: B. Lewin, *Der Diwan des ʿAbdallāh ibn al-Muʿtazz* (Istanbul, 1950), 2–3.
Dīwān (Beirut, 1381/1961), 18–19.
Muntakhab, II, 283–4.

Metre: *rajaz*.

This poem belongs to the class known as *ṭardīyāt* (hunting-poems).

1. Lewin and *Muntakhab* read *taʿarrā ufuqu l-ḍiyāʾi* ("the horizon of light became naked").

2. "Purposed to drowse": i.e. was about to sink. Lewin reads *bi-khtifāʾi* ("was about to vanish").

3. *Muntakhab* reads *ẓāhiyatan* ("proud, reddish").

4 Raising her tail like the tawny scorpion, slender, not pied as to its belly,

5 Like a black dip of a pen or a fringe of the edge of a cloak,

6 Borne along by the wings of the air, snatching its steps without any loitering,

7 And (we led forth also) a lean male dog strong of limb, contrasting with her in respect of a white hide

8 Like the track of a meteor in the sky, and knowing the difference between chiding away and calling,

9 With ears dropping pendulous like the flower of the dark-blue hyacinth,

10 With a claw like a cobbler's awl, and eyeballs little flecked with motes,

11 Pure and bright as a drop of water, gliding between the hillocks of the desert

12 As a speckled snake glides; he has spotted betwixt the mountain-side and the plain

13 A herd of antelopes pasturing their young in a remote, flowering meadow, a desolate place,

14 Dark green as the belly of an emerald snake, in it as it were the embroidery of the spotted serpent,

15 As though they were the plaits of a grizzled woman, hunting down without fatigue and weariness

16 Fifty, not less in the numbering, and he sold us flesh with blood.

---

4. "Pied as to its belly": see Lane 1872, col. 1 (of a horse, "freed from the whiteness termed *waḍaḥ*").

10. From this point there are certain additions in the text of Lewin.

11. *Dīwān* reads *tansābu*.

14. For *ka-naqshi* Lewin reads *musūku*.

٤ شائلةً كالعقرب السمراء   مُرْهَفةً مُطْلَقةَ الأحشاء

٥ كمَدَّةٍ من قلَمٍ سوداء   أو هُدْبَةٍ من طرف الرداء

٦ تَحْمِلُها أجنحةُ الهواء   تستلب الخطو بلا إبطاء

٧ ومُخْطَفًا مُوَثَّق الأعضاء   خالَفَها بجلدةٍ بيضاء

٨ كأَثَرِ الشهاب فى السماء   ويعرف الزجر من الدعاء

٩ بأُذُنٍ ساقطة الأرجاء   كوردة السوسنة الشهلاء

١٠ ذا بُرْثُنٍ كمِثْقَب الحذّاء   ومقلةٍ قليلة الأقذاء

١١ صافيةٍ كقطرة من ماء   ينساب بين أَكَمِ الصحراء

١٢ مثل انسياب حيّةٍ رقطاء   آنس بين السفح والفضاء

١٣ سِرْبَ ظباء رُتَّعِ الأطلاء   فى عازبٍ مُنَوِّرٍ خلاء

١٤ أَحْوَى كبطن الحيّة الخضراء   فيه كنقش الحيّة الرقشاء

١٥ كأنّها ضفائر الشمطاء   يصطاد قبل الأَيْنِ والعناء

١٦ خَمْسين لا تنقص فى الإحصاء   وباعَنا اللحومَ بالدماء

---

15. For *yaṣṭādu* Lewin reads *fa-ṣāda*.

16. For *tanquṣu* Lewin reads *yanquṣna*. After this couplet *Dīwān* adds five hemistichs which in Lewin form a separate poem (p. 5). "He sold us flesh with blood": the dog bleeds from the eagerness of the chase.

13 AL-MUTANABBĪ

1 According to the degree of the people of resolve come the resolutions, and according to the degree of noble men come the noble actions.

2 Small deeds are great in the eyes of the small, and great deeds are small in the eyes of the great.

3 Saif al-Daula charges the army with the burden of his own zeal, which numerous armies have proved incapable of bearing,

4 And he demands of men what he has in himself—and that is something which (even) lions do not claim.

5 The longest-living of birds, even the eagles of the desert, the young ones and the old ones of them, offer (themselves as) ransom for his armoury;

6 It would not harm them that they were created without talons, seeing that his swords and hilts have been created.

7 Does al-Ḥadath the red recognise its own colour, and does it know which of the two wine-bearers was the clouds?

8 The white clouds watered it before he descended, then when he drew near it the skulls watered it (again).

9 He built it, and built it high, whilst lances were clashing against lances and the waves of the fates surged around it;

10 The like of madness possessed it, then amulets consisting of the corpses of the slain thereafter bedecked it.

11 (It was) an exile driven away by destiny, then you restored it to the (true) religion with Khaṭṭī lances in destiny's despite.

---

13 Sources: F. Dieterici, *Mutanabbii carmina* (Berlin, 1861), 548–56.
Dīwān (ed. 'Abd al-Raḥmān al-Barqūqī, Cairo, 1348/1930), II, 269–79.
Dīwān (ed. 'Abd al-Wahhāb 'Azzām, Cairo, 1363/1944), 374–9.
Muntakhab, II, 344–6.
Nuṣūṣ, 30–2.

Metre: *ṭawīl*.

This celebrated ode was dedicated to the Ḥamdānid Saif al-Daula on his recapture of the frontier-post of al-Ḥadath in 343/954 after it had been burned in 337/948 by Bardas Phokas, see *Encycl. of Isl.*[1], II, 187.

1. Note the *jinās* and *mulā'ama*.
2. Note the *ṭibāq* and *mulā'ama*.
3. For *l-jaisha* 'Azzām reads *l-nāsa*.

١٣ المتنبّى

١ على قدر أهل العزم تأتى العزائمُ — وتأتى على قدر الكِرام المكارمُ

٢ وتعظم فى عين الصغير صغارهم — وتصغر فى عين العظيم العظائم

٣ يكلِّف سيفُ الدولة الجيشَ همَّه — وقد عجزت عنه الجيوشُ الخضارم

٤ ويطلب عند الناس ما عند نفسه — وذلك ما لا تدّعيه الضراغم

٥ يُفَدِّى أتَمُّ الطير عمراً سلاحَه — نسورُ الملا أحداثُها والقشاعم

٦ وما ضرَّها خلقٌ بغير مخالب — وقد خُلِقَتْ أسيافُه والقوائم

٧ هل الحدثُ الحمراءُ تعرف لونَها — وتعلم أىُّ الساقِيَين الغمائم

٨ سقتْها الغَمَامُ الغُرُّ قبل نزوله — فلمّا دنا منها سقتْها الجماجم

٩ بناها فأَعْلَى والقنا تقرع القنا — وموجُ المنايا حولها متلاطم

١٠ وكان بها مِثْلُ الجُنُون فأصبحت — ومن جثث القتلى عليها تمائم

١١ طريدةُ دَهْرٍ ساقها فرددتَها — على الدين بالخطّىّ والدهرُ راغم

---

5. For *l-malā* the variant *l-falā* is recorded.

6. This verse may also be construed as a question.

7. "The red": "so-called because its soil is all red" (Yāqūt, III, 231). "Which of the two wine-bearers": whether the clouds (for it had rained a few days before the battle) or the blood of the slain Byzantines.

8. The clouds are described as "white" on account of the lightning-flashes.

9. The poet refers to Saif al-Daula's reconstruction of the fortress.

10. The corpses of the slain acted as amulets which are hung upon a mad person to drive away his madness.

11. The fortress-town had been exiled from Islam by the Byzantines when they captured it.

12 You cause the nights to lose (forever) anything that you take (from them), whereas they are debtors repaying what they take from you.

13 When what you intend is a future verb (act), it becomes past tense before any conditional particles can be prefixed to it;

14 And how can the Byzantines and Russians hope to destroy it (al-Ḥadath), seeing that that thrust (of yours) is for it foundations and pillars?

15 They had summoned it to justice, and the fates were the arbiters; and no wronged man died, nor did any wronger live.

16 They came against you trailing their steel, as though they travelled by night on horses that had no feet.

17 When they flashed, their swords could not be distinguished—their garments and headgear were of the like (steel);

18 An army that marched slowly from the east of the earth and the west, confused noises proceeding from it (echoing) in the ears of the Gemini;

19 Gathered together in it was every tongue and nation, and only interpreters could make the speakers understood.

20 What a time, the time whose fire melted away the counterfeit, and all that remained was a sharp (sword) or a sturdy warrior (lion)!

21 Broken to pieces was all that could not break through armour and lances, and of the champions there fled whoever did not strike against (the enemy).

22 You stood firm, when there was no doubt that any who stood must die, as though you were in the very eyelid of death, and death was asleep,

23 The champions passing you by, wounded and in flight, whilst your face shone brightly and your mouth was smiling.

24 You surpassed the bounds of courage and reason, so that people said you had knowledge of the unseen.

---

12. The variant *akhadhnahu* (subj. *l-layālī*) is recorded, and preferred by Dieterici.

13. "Conditional particles": particles governing the jussive, i.e. before it can be said, do not do it, or, let him do otherwise.

15. Note the double *jinās*.

16. "That had no feet": the horses' feet were invisible because their black trappings reached to the ground.

١٢ تُفيتُ الليالى كلَّ شىء أخذتَه — وهنّ لما يأخذن منك غوارم

١٣ إذا كان ما تنويه فعلاً مُضارِعًا — مضى قبل أن تُلْقَى عليه الجوازم

١٤ وكيف ترجّى الروم والروس هدمَها — وذا الطعنُ آساسٌ لها ودعائم

١٥ وقد حاكموها والمنايا حواكمٌ — فما مات مظلومٌ ولا عاش ظالم

١٦ أتوك يجرّون الحديد كأنّهم — سَرَوْا بجيادٍ ما لهنّ قوائم

١٧ إذا برقوا لم تُعْرَف البِيضُ منهمُ — ثيابُهُمُ من مثلها والعمائم

١٨ خميسٌ بشرق الأرض والغرب زَحْفُه — وفى أُذُن الجوزاء منه زمازم

١٩ تَجَمَّعَ فيه كلُّ لِسْنٍ وأمّةٍ — فما تُفْهِم الحدّاثَ إلّا التراجم

٢٠ فللّه وقتٌ ذوّب الغِشَّ نارُه — فلم يَبْقَ إلّا صارمٌ أو ضُبارم

٢١ تَقَطَّعَ ما لا يقطع الدرعَ والقنا — وفَرَّ مِن الأبطال مَنْ لا يصادم

٢٢ وقفتَ وما فى الموت شكٌّ لواقفٍ — كأنّك فى جفن الردى وهو نائم

٢٣ تمرُّ بك الأبطالُ كَلْمَى هزيمةً — ووجهُك وضّاحٌ وثغرُك باسم

٢٤ تجاوزتَ مقدار الشجاعة والنُهَى — إلى قول قومٍ أنت بالغيب عالم

---

18. "Marched slowly": being so heavily accoutred.
20. Note the partial *jinās* (*al-zā'id*).
21. For *l-abṭāli* Dieterici reads *l-fursāni*. Note the *mulā'ama*.
22. "And death was asleep": its eyelids being closed, so that Saif al-Daula was completely encompassed.

25 You pressed their two wings tightly upon the heart, so that the under-feathers and wing-tips died under the squeezing,

26 With a blow that struck the crania while victory was still absent, and proceeded (forthwith) to the upper breasts as victory advanced.

27 You despised the Rudainī spears so that you flung them away, and so that it was as though the sword was reviling the lance;

28 Whoever seeks a great victory, its keys are only the light, cutting white swords.

29 You scattered them over all al-Uḥaidab, just as dirhams are scattered over a bride,

30 Your horses trampling with you the nests on the mountain-tops, and many dishes of food lay about the nests.

31 The eagles' chicks thought you visited them with their mothers, whilst they were (in reality) sturdy, noble steeds;

32 When they slipped you made them go on their bellies, as snakes crawl along on the earth's surface.

33 Does that domesticus advance (upon you) every day, his neck blaming his face for advancing?

34 Is he ignorant of the wind of the lion until he tastes it? And the wild beasts know well the wind of lions.

35 The violent onslaughts of the Amir distressed him with (the loss of) his son, and the son of his brother-in-law, and his brother-in-law.

36 He departed, thanking his companions for his having escaped the sword-edges because the latter were preoccupied with their crania and wrists

37 And understanding the voice of the Mashrafī swords about them, for all that the voices of swords are incomprehensible,

---

26. In this verse the poet describes dramatically the rapidity of the Muslims' victory.

27. Rudainī spears were accounted the best. Various explanations are offered for their being so named. The poet means that Saif al-Daula was so eager to get to close quarters that he discarded the spear.

29. Al-Uḥaidab was the name of a mountain near al-Ḥadath.

30. "Dishes of food": i.e. the bodies of the slain.

٢٥ ضممتَ جناحَيْهم على القلب ضمّةً تموت الخوافى تحتها والقوادم

٢٦ بِضَرْبٍ أتى الهاماتِ والنصرُ غائبٌ وصار إلى اللَّبّات والنصرُ قادم

٢٧ حقرتَ الرُّدَيْنيّات حتّى طرحتَها وحتّى كأنّ السيف للرمح شاتم

٢٨ ومَنْ طلب الفتحَ الجليل فإنّما مفاتيحُه البِيضُ الخفاف الصوارم

٢٩ نثرتَهمُ فوق الأُحَيْدِبِ كلّه كما نُثرت فوق العروس الدراهم

٣٠ تدوس بك الخيلُ الوكورَ على الذُّرَى وقد كثرتْ حول الوكور المطاعم

٣١ تظنّ فراخُ الفُتْخ أنّك زرتها بأمّاتها وهى العتاقُ الصلادم

٣٢ إذا زلقتْ مشّيتَها ببطونها كما تَتَمَشَّى فى الصعيد الأراقم

٣٣ أفى كلّ يوم ذا الدُّمُسْتُقُ مُقْدِمٌ قفاه على الإقدام للوجه لائم

٣٤ أيُنكر ريحَ الليث حتّى يذوقه وقد عرفتْ ريحَ الليوث البهائم

٣٥ وقد فجعتْه بابنه وابن صهره وبالصهر حملاتُ الأمير الغواشم

٣٦ مضى يشكر الأصحابَ فى فوته الظبى بما شغلتْها هامُهم والمعاصم

٣٧ ويفهم صوتَ المشرفيّة فيهمِ على أنّ أصوات السيوف أعاجم

---

33. "Domesticus": "titulus praefecti earum regionum quae Hellesponto ab oriente sunt" (Freytag, II, 56). "His neck blaming his face": his neck would prefer to be retreating, and so avoiding certain defeat.

34. The wild beasts take cover when they catch the scent of a lion. The domesticus is more stupid, in that he ignored the scent (fame) of the lion he was facing, i.e. Saif al-Daula.

36. Dieterici and ʿAzzām prefer the reading *limā* for *bimā*.

37. Mashrafī swords were highly esteemed; various explanations are offered for their name.

38 Rejoiced by what he yielded to you, not out of ignorance but rather that, being despoiled, he escaped from you (as) a spoiler.

39 And you are not a monarch who routed his peer, but you were monotheism routing polytheism,

40 (A monarch) in whom all ʿAdnān was ennobled, not Rabīʿa (alone), in whom the whole world boasts, not the capitals (only).

41 Yours is the praise in regard to the pearl which I spit out; you were the giver of it, and I the arranger,

42 And it is your gifts that race with me into the battle—so that I am not blameworthy, neither are you regretful—

43 (Riding) upon every flying (steed) that (rushes) to the fray on its feet whenever the shouts (of the warriors) fall upon its ears.

44 O sword who are never sheathed, concerning which no one is in doubt and against which no one gives immunity!

45 Rejoice, smiting of crania, and glory, and elevation, and those who put their hopes in you, and Islam, that you are safe!

46 And why should the Merciful not protect your two edges as He has done, seeing that through you He ever splits the skulls of the enemy?

14 ABŪ FIRĀS

1 Ladies, have you no reward for one whose actions are good, and will you not accept the repentance of one who has acted evilly?

2 He whose passion is possessed by a fair maiden has indeed lost the way, and he who is at the mercy of a full-breasted virgin is truly abject.

---

38. The reading *min* is preferred to *ʿan* by Dieterici and ʿAzzām. "(As) a spoiler": by fleeing the domesticus despoiled Saif al-Daula of his life.

40. ʿAdnān was said to be the ancestor of all the northern Arabs, including the Banū Rabīʿa.

41. "The pearl": i.e. the verses of the poem.

42. "Your gifts": the noble horses, traditionally included in the royal bounty.

44. The variants *lasta* for *laisa* and *minka* for *minhu* are preferred by Dieterici and ʿAzzām.

45. For the construction of *hanīʾan* see Lane 2903, col. 2.

46. "Your two edges": appropriate to the name of Saif ("Sword") al-Daula.

٣٨ يُسَرُّ بما أعطاك لا عن جهالة   ولكنّ مغنومًا نجا منك غانم

٣٩ ولستَ مليكًا هازمًا لنظيره   ولكنّك التوحيدُ للشرك هازم

٤٠ تَشَرَّفُ عدنانٌ به لا ربيعةٌ   وتفتخر الدنيا به لا العواصم

٤١ لك الحمدُ فى الدرّ الذى لِىَ لفظُه   فإنّك مُعطيه وإنّىَ ناظم

٤٢ وإنّى لتعدو بى عطاياك فى الوغى   فلا أنا مذمومٌ ولا أنت نادم

٤٣ على كلّ طيّارٍ إليها برجله   إذا وقعتْ فى مسمعَيْه الغماغم

٤٤ ألا أيّها السيف الذى ليس مُغْمَدًا   ولا فيه مرتابٌ ولا منه عاصم

٤٥ هنيئًا لضرب الهام والمجد والعُلَى   وراجيك والإسلامِ أنّك سالم

٤٦ ولِمَ لا يقى الرحمنُ حدَّيْك ما وقى   وتفليقُه هامَ العِدا بك دائم

١٤ أبو فراس

١ أما لجميلٍ عندكنّ ثوابُ   ولا لمُسىءٍ عندكنّ متابُ

٢ لقد ضل من تحوى هواه خريدةٌ   وقد ذلّ من تقضى عليه كعابُ

---

14 Sources: *Dīwān* (ed. Sami Dahan, Damascus, 1944), II, 22–4.
Dīwān (Beirut, 1389/1959), 24–7.
Muntakhab, II, 359.
B. Bustānī, *Jawāhir al-adab* (Harissa, 1931), V, 115–17.

Metre: *ṭawīl.*

This poem is one of a group composed during the poet's captivity in Constantinople from 351/962 to 355/966.

1. The poem opens with a conventional amatory prelude. Note the *ṭibāq* and *mulā'ama.*

2. Note the *jinās* (*lāḥiq*) and *mulā'ama.*

3 But I, praise be to God, am a resolute man; I am invincible, when the necks (of other men) submit to them,

4 And the lovely woman does not own my heart entirely, not though she is wrapped around in tenderness and youth.

5 I run, but I do not give passion the excess of my leading-rope; I flurry, but the right course is not hidden from me.

6 When a friend breaks with you for no other cause but weariness, no reproach is appropriate to him, but separation;

7 When I do not find in one pasture what I am looking for, then I firmly resolve and ride forth to another.

8 There is no separation, so long as I am able (to prevent it); but if separation occurs in any circumstance, then there is no return (for me).

9 (I am) a long-suffering man, even if not so much as a last remnant of me remains; (I am) bold to speak, even though the sword be the answer;

10 Serene whilst the accidents of time catch at me, and death comes and goes about me.

11 I perceive the circumstances of time with an eye that sees truth as true and falsehood as falsehood.

12 In whom shall a man trust in what befalls him, and whence shall the noble free-man find companions,

13 Seeing that all mankind here, apart from the least number of them, have become wolves with (sheep's) clothing on their bodies?

14 I have feigned unmindfulness of my own people, and they deem me stupid; pebbles and dust be on the crown of the more stupid of us!

15 Had they known me as truly as I know them, then they would have been aware that I was present (in mind), and themselves absent.

16 Not every doer is requited for his deed, and not every sayer is answered by me;

---

3. Note the *ṭibāq*.

5. Sc. I keep a rein on my passion. Note the *mulā'ama*. Dahan reads *wa-lā* for *fa-lā*.

7. *Jawāhir* reads *baldatin* for *khullatin*.

٣ ولكنّني والحمد للّه حازمٌ — أعِزّ اذا ذَلَّتْ لهنّ رقابُ

٤ ولا تملك الحسناء قلبيَ كلّه — وإن شملتْها رقّةٌ وشبابُ

٥ وأجري فلا أعطي الهوى فضل مِقْوَدي — وأهفو ولا يخفى عليّ صوابُ

٦ اذا الخِلُّ لم يهجرك إلّا ملالةً — فليس له الّا الفراقَ عتابُ

٧ اذا لم أجد من خُلّةٍ ما أريده — فعندي لأخرى عزمة وركابُ

٨ وليس فراقٌ ما ٱستطعتُ فإن يكن — فراقٌ على حالٍ فليس إيابُ

٩ صَبُورٌ ولو لم تبق منّي بقيّةٌ — قَؤُولٌ ولو أنّ السيوفَ جوابُ

١٠ وَقُورٌ وأحداثُ الزمان تنوشني — وللموت حولي جَيْئَةٌ وذهابُ

١١ وأَلْحَظُ أحوال الزمان بمقلة — بها الصدق صدقٌ والكذاب كذابُ

١٢ بمن يثق الإنسان فيما ينوبه — ومن أين للحُرّ الكريم صحابُ

١٣ وقد صار هذا الناس الّا أقِلَّهم — ذِئَابًا على أجسادهن ثيابُ

١٤ تغابيتُ عن قومي فظنّوا غباوتي — بمفرق أغبانا حصىً وترابُ

١٥ ولو عرفوني حقَّ معرفتي بهم — اذاً علموا أنّي شهدتُ وغابُوا

١٦ وما كلّ فعّال يُجَازَى بفعله — ولا كلّ قوّالٍ لدىّ يُجَابُ

---

8. Note the *ṭibāq*.
14. Dahan reads *ghabāwatan*. Note the *jinās* (*al-ishtiqāq*).
15. Note the *ṭibāq*.
16. Note the *ṭibāq* and *mulā'ama*.

17 Many a speech has passed over my ears as a fly that buzzes in the noonday air.

18 To God I complain, that we are dwelling in abodes where dogs lord it over their lions.

19 The nights pass, and there is no place where I may look for profit, no quarter where I may petition for bounty.

20 No saddle is bound for me on the back of a strong galloper, neither is any tent pitched for me in the desert;

21 No trenchant blades flash for me in the encounter, no javelins shine for me in the wars.

22 Numair, ʻĀmir, Kaʻb and Kilāb in all their circumstances will remember my exploits.

23 I was the neighbour whose provision was never slow in coming to them, neither was the door of any vicissitude barred to my wealth;

24 I did not seek to attain any abuse of them, nor was my shame exposed to any seeker.

25 If I assaulted, yet my love was fixed in their breasts; or if I was clement to the foolhardy of them, for all that I was feared.

26 Cousins! what shall the sword do in the fray when its point and edge are blunted?

27 Cousins! Do not deny the truth; we are indeed harsh and hard against other than abjectness.

28 Cousins! we are the forearms and the sword-blades; one day soon there will be a coming to blows.

29 Surely men whose son is not as their sister's son are worthy to be given the verdict, and treated with awe!

30 With what excuse, when they were invoked and you were invoked, did you refuse, cousins, whilst they responded?

31 I do not claim what God knows other than it (to be true)—the courts of ʻAlī are wide open to the seekers after bounty,

32 And his actions to the desirous are generous, and his wealth to the petitioners is (free as) booty.

---

18. For the poetic licence see Wright, II, 387D.

20. "Galloper": lit. "swimmer".

21. Note the *jinās* (*mushābih*).

22. The poet lists the names of famous Arab tribes. For this meaning of *ʻillāt* see Lane 2124.

24. Note the *jinās*.

١٧ ورُبَّ كلامٍ مرَّ فوق مسامعى كما طنّ فى لُوح الهجير ذُبابُ

١٨ الى اللّه أشكو أنّنا بمنازلٍ تَحَكَّمُ فى آسادهنّ كلابُ

١٩ تمرّ الليالى ليس للنفع موضعٌ لدىّ ولا للمُعْتَفين جَنابُ

٢٠ ولا شُدّ لى سَرْجٌ على ظهر سابحٍ ولا ضُربت لى بالعراء قبابُ

٢١ ولا برقتْ لى فى اللقاء قواطعٌ ولا لمعت لى فى الحروب حِرابُ

٢٢ ستذكر أيّامى نُمَيْرٌ وعَامِرٌ وكَعْبٌ على عِلّاتها وكلابُ

٢٣ أنا الجار لا زادى بطىءٌ عليهمُ ولا دون مالى للحوادث بابُ

٢٤ ولا أطلب العوراء منهم أصيبها ولا عورتى للطالبين تصابُ

٢٥ وأسطو وحبّى ثابتٌ فى صدورهم وأحلم عن جهّالهم وأهابُ

٢٦ بنى عمّنا ما يصنع السيف فى الوغى إذا فُلّ منه مَضْرِبٌ وذُبابُ

٢٧ بنى عمّنا لا تُنكروا الحقّ إنّنا شدادٌ على غير الهوان صلابُ

٢٨ بنى عمّنا نحن السواعد والظبى ويوشك يوماً أن يكون ضرابُ

٢٩ وإنّ رجالاً ما ابنهم كابن أختهم حريّون أن يُقْضَى لهم ويُهابُوا

٣٠ فعن أىّ عذرٍ إن دُعُوا ودُعيتمُ أبيتم بنى أعمامنا وأجابُوا

٣١ وما أدّعى ما يعلم اللّه غيره رحابُ علىٍّ للعُفاة رحابُ

٣٢ وأفعاله للراغبين كريمة وأمواله للطالبين نهابُ

---

25. Note the *ṭibāq* and *mulā'ama*.

26. "Cousins": Abū Firās was a Ḥamdānid, a cousin of Saif al-Daula on whose title he here puns.

31. Note the *jinās*. 'Alī is the proper name of Saif al-Daula.

32. Note the perfect *mulā'ama*.

33 But a sword in my hands glanced off from him, and a meteor from him was dark in my eyes,

34 And he was slow to (answer) me, and the fates are swift, and death has nails and claws that shed blood unavenged.

35 Now even if there were not an ancient love for us to reckon, nor a close relationship between men,

36 Yet Islam is better guarded by his not wasting me, and I can defend Islam and be his deputy in doing so.

37 But I am content under all circumstances that it may be known which of the two conditions is right and just,

38 And I continue to be content with a little affection on his part, there being a veil intervening between much,

39 And to seek his land, to secure the continuance of his love, whilst my recollection in another land is the desire and demand (of its inhabitants).

40 So it is with pure love—no reward is to be hoped for on its account, neither punishment feared because of it.

41 I used to fear banishment when the bonds of union joined us together, and when every day we met and spoke;

42 So how (much the more now), seeing that the realm of Caesar lies between us, and the sea surges and tosses around me?

43 What? After I have sacrificed myself for your desires, am I to be rewarded, when I am rewarded, with the bitterness of reproach?

44 Would that you were sweet, when life is bitter, and would that you were satisfied, when (all other) men are angry!

45 And would that that which is between us were flourishing, and what is between me and all the worlds were a desolation!

---

33. The poet means that his sharp entreaty failed to pierce Saif al-Daula's heart; his favourable regard was therefore denied to him. Note the *ṭibāq* and *mulā'ama*.

35. For *nu'iddubu* Dahan reads *'ahidtubu*.

36. Note the *jinās*. Dahan reads *'anka* for *'anbu*.

37. "The two conditions": i.e. whether Saif al-Daula accords his favour or disfavour.

38. Note the *ṭibāq*.

٣٣ ولكن نبا منه بكفّيَ صارم   وأظلم فى عينيّ منه شهابُ

٣٤ وأبطأ عنّى والمنايا سريعةٌ   وللموت ظُفْرٌ قد أطلّ ونابُ

٣٥ فإن لم يكن وُدٌّ قديمٌ نعدّه   ولا نسبٌ بين الرجال قُرابُ

٣٦ فأَحْوَطُ للإسلام أن لا يُضيعَنى   ولى عنه فيه حوطةٌ ومنابُ

٣٧ ولكنّنى راضٍ على كلّ حالةٍ   ليُعْلَمَ أىّ الحالتَيْنِ صوابُ

٣٨ وما زلتُ أرضى بالقليل محبّةً   لديه وما دون الكثير حجابُ

٣٩ وأطلب إبقاءً على الودّ أرْضَه   وذكرى مُنىً فى غيرها وطلابُ

٤٠ كذاك الوداد المحض لا يُرْتَجَى له   ثوابٌ ولا يُخْشَى عليه عقابُ

٤١ وقد كنتُ أخشى الهجر والشملُ جامعٌ   وفى كلّ يوم لقية وخطابُ

٤٢ فكيف وفيما بيننا ملك قيصرٍ   وللبحر حولى زخرة وعُبَابُ

٤٣ أمِنْ بعد بذل النفس فيما تريده   أُثاب بمُرّ العتب حين أُثابُ

٤٤ فلَيْتَك تحلو والحياة مريرةٌ   وليتك ترضى والأنام غِضابُ

٤٥ وليت الذى بينى وبينك عامرٌ   وبينى وبين العالمين خرابُ

---

39. "In another land": the reference is to *v.* 29.

40. Note the *ṭibāq*. After this verse Dahan inserts

wa-mā ana bi-l-bāghī ʿalā l-ḥubbi rashwatan
ḍaʿīfu hawan yubghā ʿalaihi thawābu

44. Note the double *ṭibāq*.

45. Note the *ṭibāq*. Dahan adds two further couplets.

15 AL-SHARĪF AL-RAḌĪ

1 O sickness of your heart, deriving from a lightning-flash which illuminates and (then) is extinguished

2 Over the eastern part of Nejd—a pasture barren to your eyes—

3 Just as a forearm flashes, having upon it a bracelet of pure gold,

4 As if it were a fire on a high hill kindled into flame for the guests

5 Or sparks displayed, when the long-tressed night is pitch-dark,

6 By a man plying with his hands as he bends over the flint-stick,

7 Or a mistress of a house whose incense is moist upon the fire.

8 The hollow, containing Maʿān and ʿĀqil and al-Haḍb,

9 Is filled with the rumble of a thunder whereby the flock (of gazelles) is startled,

10 And lightning flashes, like arrows splitting the dust (of battle).

11 Do you not see the lightning appearing?—except that your eyes are clouded with tears

12 And sighs blow a sandstorm amidst your ribs—

13 Illuminating a grave at al-Ṭaff wherein lies the most precious and most beloved.

14 That grave is filled with water of the eyes, or rather with the diaphragm of the heart.

15 Never did I think that one day—and destiny strikes variously—

16 I should pass the night with a wide desert between me and meeting you,

---

15 Source: *Dīwān* (Beirut, 1380/1961), I, 159–64.
Metre: *mujtathth*.
This poem was composed by al-Sharīf al-Raḍī on receiving news of the death of his sister.

1. The poet commences with a conventional "desert Arab" opening scene of lightning viewed in the distance. For *dīn* in the meaning of "sickness" (the meaning "constant rain" is also relevant) see Lane 944, col. 3.

2. Note the pun on the literal and metaphorical meanings of *marʿan*.

١٥ الشريف الرضى

١ يا دين قلبك من با   رق يُنير ويخبو

٢ على شريقيّ نَجْد   مرعىً لعينك جَدْبُ

٣ كما تُليحُ ذِراعٌ   فيها من النضر قُلْبُ

٤ كأنّه نارُ عليا   ءَ للضيوف تُشَبُّ

٥ أو ساطعاتٌ أراها   والليلُ داجٍ أَزَبُّ

٦ مُراوِحٌ بيدَيْه   على الزناد مُكِبُّ

٧ أو أُمُّ مَشْوًى يلنجو   جُها على النار رَطْبُ

٨ الغَوْرُ منه مَعانٌ   وعاقلٌ والهَضْبُ

٩ له حفيفُ رعادٍ   يُراعُ منه السِّرْبُ

١٠ وبارقاتٌ كما شقّ   ت العجاجَ القَضْبُ

١١ أما ترى البرق يبدو   إلّا لعينك غَرْبُ

١٢ وللزفير هبابٌ   بين الضلوع وهَبُّ

١٣ يُضيءُ بالطفّ قبراً   فيه الأَعَزُّ الأَحَبُّ

١٤ فيه من العين ماءٌ   لا بل من القلب خَلْبُ

١٥ ما كنتُ أحسب يوماً   والدهرُ ضَرْبٌ وضَرْبُ

١٦ أنّى أَبيتُ وبيني   وبين لقياك سَهْبُ

---

3. The comparison of lightning with human hands was first established by Imra' al-Qais in his *Mu'allaqa*, see my *The Seven Odes*, 66. The image is here cleverly refined.

4. The poet refers to the fire lit to guide night-travellers to shelter and hospitality.

8. For Ma'ān, see Yāqūt, VIII, 93; for 'Āqil, see Yāqūt, VI, 97; for al-Haḍb, see Yāqūt, VIII, 466–7.

13. "A grave at al-Ṭaff": a locality near Kufa where al-Ḥusain the son of 'Alī b. Abī Ṭalib was slain, see Yāqūt, VI, 51.

17 And that oblique gales would drive us apart

18 To where white wild cows and onagers pasture;

19 And how should sand-grouse coming to water sip and swallow there?

20 Abode of my people! Where are they who halted in your quarter,

21 Stallions (of men) broken by the hands of doom, so that they fled

22 Driven on by an erect driver of the fates

23 Impelling onwards deep-rooted trunks, even if they are remiss or procrastinate.

24 They were swords—when they beheld the warrior, they rushed—

25 And Zāghibī lances—if they were pointed from the abode, they protected:

26 Dwellings in which they abode were a security for the people, and a terror

27 In (vainly assailing) which spears and lean horses were worn out—

28 The spear-point streaming, the slender charger fined down to a shadow—

29 Judgement concluding in firm resolve, and generosity coming not seldom.

30 Every day the proud and arrogant of us becomes obedient,

31 The stock of the towering leafy tree is lopped, the issue dies childless.

32 Neither the hated of the people remains (immortal), nor the revered and beloved—

33 Alike in the cavern of death are the sleek and sound of back and the scabby ones.

34 Fate proceeds on its way, and both doctor and patient depart.

35 How long is that security, seeing that the accidents of fortune plunder and drag away

---

31. "Dies childless": reading *yadruju* for *yudraḥu* ("is driven away").

١٧ وأن تطاردَ ما بَيْـ … نَنا زعازع نُكْبُ

١٨ بحيث يرتع أُدْمٌ … من الجوازى وحُقْبُ

١٩ وكيف يكرعُ مُسْتَو … رِدُ القطا ويَعُبُّ

٢٠ يا دار قوسِىَّ أين الـ … أولى بربعك لَبُّوا

٢١ مَصَاعِبٌ حطمتْهم … أيدى المنون فَجَبُّوا

٢٢ يسوقُهم للمقادير … رسائقُ مُتْلَئِبُّ

٢٣ مُقَحِّمٌ للجراثيـ … م إن وَنَوا أو أَغَبُّوا

٢٤ كانوا السيوفَ اذا عا … ينوا المقاتلَ هَبُّوا

٢٥ والزاغبيّاتِ إن أشْـ … رِعُوا عن الدار ذَبُّوا

٢٦ مَنَازِلٌ كان فيها … للقوم أَمْنٌ ورُعْبُ

٢٧ تُكَدُّ فيها الأنابيـ … بُ والرباطُ القُبُّ

٢٨ يهمى السنانُ ويُسْتَضْـ … مَرُ الجوادُ الأَقَبُّ

٢٩ رَأْىٌ يَغُبُّ لِحَزْمٍ … ونَائِلٌ لا يَغُبُّ

٣٠ ينقاد فى كلّ يوم … منّا الأَبِىُّ الصَّعْبُ

٣١ يُجَدُّ أصلُ وريق الـ … ذُّرَى ويدْرُجُ عَقْبُ

٣٢ لا مبغض القوم يبقى … ولا المجلُّ المحبُّ

٣٣ سواءٌ المُلْسُ فى غا … رة الرَّدَى والجُرْبُ

٣٤ يجرى القضاءُ ويمضى … الطبيبُ والمُسْتَطِبُّ

٣٥ كم ذا الأمانُ ولـلـنـا … ئبات سَلْبٌ وجَذْبُ

36 And their ravens are ever croaking and cawing to presage departure?

37 The peace of the nights deludes, for their peace is (really) war.

38 Fate crouches threateningly against us, and leaps—

39 One day (fair) delusion, and one day rushing upon us and mischiefing,

40 Making for the narrow pass, whilst the broad highway lies before.

41 Is the end of playing earnestness, or is the end of earnestness playing?

42 My sister! a calamity that assailed you was a calamity indeed,

43 And a misfortune which struck me down, being far from you, was hard to bear.

44 An arrow smote you, the notch and edge of which belonged to destiny;

45 Its head did not miss the mark ever, nor were its feathers ill-trimmed.

46 After you, grief and distress are my bedfellows

47 Even as, after the hump has been hacked off, the roast remains all night on the fire.

48 How should the side find repose upon the pebbles of care?

49 If thrusting and striking could have repelled from you the hasty fates

50 A sharp lance-point would have penetrated into them, and a keen sword hit (the joint),

51 And sturdy-armed, thick-necked men would have stood in the way of doom,

52 And wolves of the night would have walked warily with the tall spears.

53 You finished a term of life, after which a term of glory came to an end.

54 The only suitor you had was of the fates;

55 Now before every veil of chastity (other) veils are (hung),

55. "(Other) veils": sc. the winding-shroud.

٣٦ وبالزيال لغِرْبا   نِها شحيجٌ ونَعْبُ
٣٧ يَغُرُّ سِلْمُ الليالى   والسلمُ منهنّ حَرْبُ
٣٨ لنا من الدهر رَبْضٌ   على وعيدٍ وَوَثْبُ
٣٩ يوماً غرورٌ ويوماً   عَدْوٌ علينا وشَغْبُ
٤٠ ينحو المضيقَ وقد أعْـ   ـرَضَ الطريقُ اللَّحْبُ
٤١ أآخرُ اللعب جِدٌّ   أم آخر الجدّ لِعْبُ
٤٢ شقيقتى إنّ خَطْباً   عدا عليك لَخَطْبُ
٤٣ وإنّ رُزْءاً رمانى   بالبعد عنك لَصَعْبُ
٤٤ سَهْمٌ أصابك منه   للقدر فُوقٌ وغَرْبُ
٤٥ لا النصل منه بنابٍ   يوماً ولا الريشُ لَغْبُ
٤٦ يبيتُ بعدك فى مضـ   ـجعى الجوى والكَرْبُ
٤٧ كما يبيت رسيضٌ   بعد السنام الأَجَبُّ
٤٨ أنَّى على قضض الهـ   ـمّ يطمئنّ الجَنْبُ
٤٩ لو ردّ عنك المنايا الـ   ـعجالَ طَعْنٌ وضَرْبُ
٥٠ لخاض فيها سِنَانٌ   ماضٍ وطَبَّقَ عَضْبُ
٥١ وقام دون الردى غُلْـ   ـظُ السواعد غُلْبُ
٥٢ وناقلت بالعوالى   ذُؤْبانُ ليلٍ تخُبُّ
٥٣ قضيتِ نحبًا قضى بعـ   ـده من المجد نَحْبُ
٥٤ ولم يكن لك إلاّ   من المقادير خَطْبُ
٥٥ ودون كلّ حجابٍ   من العفافة حُجْبُ

56 And your grave is a preservation before any mate should embrace you.

57 It is as though every day my heart yearns more strongly for you,

58 And as soon as the wound is healed, a fresh scar is formed on my heart.

59 The falling of my glance is weary of other than you, and grows dim.

60 I reverence your grave too much to say, "May the riders greet it!"

61 Or to say, "May the persisting shower of the rain-cloud water it"—

62 Except for the need of a soul that longs and hankers for you—

63 Or that any athirst should be assuaged, if a draught drenches your grave;

64 And how should a grave thirst that possesses (such) sweet, pure water,

65 Or how should a land be darkened where the stars of heaven are veiled?

66 (A land) whose flowers are glory, not the basil of the hills and the dried-up barley-grass.

67 You have come to dwell near a neighbour who has received you with affection and love.

68 It is a watercourse, but a watercourse belonging to God and the angels.

69 O what a sleep! then arising from it unto Paradise.

70 If the bodily form is afar, yet the links (of affection) are near.

71 I visit it infrequently, and in spite of me the visitation is infrequent.

72 If the eye is empty of you, yet the heart has been filled with you;

73 And if you have set, yet the rising (stars) also have their east and their west.

74 Blame passed away from you, and Fate has blame and reviling on account of you,

---

56. "Any mate": reading *tirbu* for *turbu*.

64. "That possesses (such) sweet, pure water": i.e. the saliva of the beautiful woman.

٥٦ وقبـرك الصونُ من قبـ   ـل أن يضمّك تربُ

٥٧ كأنّني كل يوم   قلبي اليك أُصَبُّ

٥٨ وكلّما اندمل القر   حُ عاد قلبي نَدْبُ

٥٩ يَكِلُّ واقعُ طرفي   عمّن سواك وينبو

٦٠ أُجِلُّ قبرك عن أن   أقول حيّاه رَكْبُ

٦١ أو أن أقول سقاه   صَوْبُ الغمام المُرِبُّ

٦٢ إلّا لحاجةِ نفس   تهفو اليك وتصبو

٦٣ أو أن يُبَلَّ غليل   إن بَلَّ قبرك شرْبُ

٦٤ وكيف يَظْمَأُ قَبْرٌ   فيه الزلالُ العَذْبُ

٦٥ أم كيف تُظْلِمُ أرْضٌ   أُجِنَّ فيها الشُّهْبُ

٦٦ نوّارها المجدُ لا حَزْ   وَةُ الرُّبَى والعِرْبُ

٦٧ جاورتِ جاراً تلقّا   ك منه بِرٌّ وحُبُّ

٦٨ شِعْبٌ غدا وَهْوَ للّـ   ـه والملائك شِعْبُ

٦٩ يا نومةً ثُمَّ منها   الى الجنان المَهَبُّ

٧٠ إن كان للشخص بُعْدٌ   فللعلائق قُرْبُ

٧١ أُغِبُّه وبرغْمي   إنّ الزيارة غِبُّ

٧٢ لئن خلا منك طَرْفٌ   لقد مُلي منك قَلْبُ

٧٣ وإن غربت فللطّا   لعاتِ شَرْقٌ وغَرْبُ

٧٤ خلاك ذَمٌّ وذَمٌّ   للدهر فيك وقَضْبُ

---

67. "Affection and love": in the *Dīwān* there is a misprint.

75 And even after my today I continue to reproach Fate.

76 So how long shall I pass the night, with this sin that the fates have committed against me?

16 MIHYĀR AL-DAILAMĪ

1 Do you know, daughter of the Persians, how many there are who reproach your brother regarding (his) passion,

2 Proceeding to revile him with a bland countenance which speaks out of an envious and spiteful heart?

3 Whilst he proceeds straight upon his path along with glory, as straight as the sharp Mashrafī sword,

4 Following the example laid down for him by his fathers—and the lion-cubs are the very likeness of the lions—

5 Being of a thicket, no branch of which, ever since Persia planted it, has bent pliantly to (the hand of) any prover.

6 To whom on the earth, which was (once) a dense forest, belong buildings not fit for any to demolish?

7 Who slew falsehood with the truth, and who humbled the oppressor to the oppressed

8 Except the Sons of Sāsān, or their grandfathers? How swift in flight were their wing-feathers and pinions!

9 Which of them shed more tears of blood? For every one of them is too sublime for my coursing tears.

10 How much their recollection has tugged at my fortitude, as one departed tugs at the heart of the distracted lover!

11 No wonder, seeing that the world was fragrant with them, when after them it has not been sweet for one day to the taster.

12 No tribe ever contended with me concerning them, but that I proved a choking mouthful to the adversary,

---

76. Reading *ladai* for *li-dhī*.

16 Source: *Dīwān* (Cairo, 1349/1930), III, 334–6.
Metre: *rajaz*.
This poem is an expression of the Persian and Shī'ite attitude.

1. The poet begins with an amatory prelude in the form of an address to his

٧٥ ولم يزل بعد يومى مِنّى على الدهر عَتْبُ

٧٦ فكم أبيتُ وعندى لَدَى المقادير ذَنْبُ

١٦ مهيار الديلمى

١ أتعلمين يآبنةَ الأعاجم كم لأخيك فى الهوى من لائم

٢ يُهَبُّ يلحاه بوجهٍ طَلْقٍ ينطق عن قلب حسودٍ راغم

٣ وهْو مع المجد على سبيله ماضٍ مضاءَ المشرفىّ الصارم

٤ ممتثلاً ما سنَّه آباؤه إنّ الشبول شَبَهُ الضراغم

٥ من أيكةٍ مذ غرستْها فارسٌ ما لان غمزاً فرعُها لعاجم

٦ لمن على الأرض وكانت غَيْضَةً أبنيةٌ لا تُبتغَى لهادم

٧ مَنْ فَرَسَ الباطلَ بالحقّ ومن أرغم للمظلوم أنفَ الظالم

٨ إلّا بنو ساسانَ أو جدودُهم طِرْ بخوافيهم وبالقوادم

٩ أيّهمُ أبكَى دماً فكلُّهم يجِلُّ عن دموعىَ السواجم

١٠ كم جذبتْ ذكراهمُ من جَلَدى جذب الفريق من فؤاد الهائم

١١ لا غروَ والدنيا بهم طابت اذا لم تحلُ يوماً بعدهم لطاعم

١٢ ما اختصمتنى فيهمُ قبيلةٌ إلّا وكنتُ غُصّةَ المخاصم

Persian sister. The "passion" is to be understood as his devotion to the 'Alid cause; he was a pupil of al-Sharīf al-Raḍī.

5. "No branch": the image of the spear-tester is conventional for proof of firm resolution. Mihyār opens his Shu'ūbī argument of the superiority of the Persians over the Arabs. Note the pun implicit in *li-'ājimi*.

7. Note the pun on the use of *farasa*.

13 Neither did I publish their excellence upon my hand, without I scattered the whole necklace of the arranger.

14 If men should deny their sublimity, wherefore should a garden disown the benefits of the clouds?

15 Or is the sword buckled on any but its master, seeing that only his hand fits the hilt of it?

16 If you are just, he has best right to the earth who adorned it with noble resolves.

17 You who falsely attribute their glory to yourselves, puff away—the eye of the dreamer is the proper place for nightmares!

18 There is a difference between a head in which a crown takes pride, and heads that take pride in turbans!

19 How often their swords on behalf of their neighbours foreshortened the steps of time, hilt upon hilt!

20 And their defenders protected against great calamities that were put to flight by great exploits,

21 And conferred benefits, and snatched the greater part of liberality from the right hand of every one who took it upon himself to pay—

22 Noble qualities which unstitched what you have patched together out of the might of ʻAmr and the liberality of Ḥātim.

23 Your world was yet in darkness, till it was lit up by a star in the (House of) Hāshim

24 By which you became visible, and before that you were a secret dying in the breast of a concealer.

25 Through his guidance and good fortune you dwelt, after hollows, on the heights of great capitals.

26 Indeed, had they a liberal monarch upon whom you can call? Had they a contender of a monarch?

27 Your banners fluttered victorious, when you armoured yourselves with his name in the affray.

---

12. Note the *jinās*.

13. Note the *ṭibāq*. The poet boasts of his superiority over the rhyming productions of the Sunnī propagandists.

17. "Nightmares": a farrago of fantasies, see Koran, XII, 44.

١٣ ولا نشرتُ فى يدى فضلَهمُ   إلّا نثرتُ ملءَ عِقْدِ الناظم

١٤ إن يجحد الناسُ عُلاهم فبما   أنكرَ روضٌ نِعَمَ الغمائم

١٥ أو قُلِّدَ الصارمُ غيرَ ربّه   فليس غيرُ كفّه للقائم

١٦ أَحَقُّ بالأرض اذا أنصفتمُ   عامرُها بشرفِ العزائم

١٧ يا ناحلى مجدهمُ أنفسَهم   هُبُّوا فللأضغاث عين الحالم

١٨ شتّان رأسٌ يفخر التاج به   وأروسٌ تفخر بالعمائم

١٩ كم قصّرت سيوفهم عن جارهم   خُطَى الزمان قائماً بقائم

٢٠ ودفعتْ حُماتُهم عن نُوَبٍ   عظائمٍ تُكْشَفُ بالعظائم

٢١ وخَوَّلوا من نعمةٍ واغتنموا   جُلَّ السماح عن يمين غارم

٢٢ مناقبٌ تَفْتُقُ ما رقّعتمُ   من بأس عمرو وسماح حاتم

٢٣ ما برحتْ مظلمةً دنياكمُ   حتّى أضاء كوكبٌ فى هاشم

٢٤ بِنتم به وكنتمُ من قبله   سرًّا يموت فى ضلوع كاتم

٢٥ حللتمُ بهديه ويمنه   بعد الوهاد فى ذُرى العواصم

٢٦ وعادِ هل من مالكٍ مسامحٍ   تدعون هل من مالكٍ مقاوم

٢٧ تخفق راياتُكمُ منصورةً   اذا ادّرعتم باسمه فى جاحم

---

22. Mihyār challenges the supremacy in their respective virtues of two heroes of the Jāhilīya.
23. "In the (House of) Hāshim": the tribe to which the Prophet belonged.
26. For this use of *'ādi*, see Lane 2189, col. 3.

28 He was given to live in hardship at your hands, whose history in the accounts of the battles is a disgrace to you,

29 Some of you slain doing battle, unbelieving, some in hypocritical truce.

30 Then he died, preserved from doubt, but not secure from your treachery.

31 You broke his covenants regarding his family, and swerved from the highway of (his) ordinances.

32 You also witnessed the slaying of his cousin, the best man of prayer and fasting after him,

33 And (you witnessed) how your leader Yazīd sinfully deemed fit at al-Ṭaff to shed the blood of the son of Fāṭima;

34 And so until today, the young fawns are crimsoning with his blood the talons of vultures.

35 And the Persians, when they embraced his religion—the hand of no severer attained (to cut) the bond.

36 Who then is worthier to rule that bond, dedicated to eternal bliss?

37 Inevitably one day shall be repaired a slip committed by an outstripper, an error committed by a resolute man.

38 Were the wind to blow a fresh breeze forever, refuge would not be secured from the mischief of the simooms,

39 Nor would a beautiful woman be secure the whole of her life from some evil eye, being in need of amulets.

40 You who envy me, receive a grief between your sides which will hurl burning coals upon your heart,

41 And be content, for I have eluded you, not obscure in ignominy, (leaving you) to gnash the teeth of regret.

42 May you continue ever ill-fortuned as to reward, trembling (in return) for one tranquil, and sleepless for one who slumbers!

---

32. "His cousin": the fourth caliph 'Alī ibn Abī Ṭalib.
33. The reference is to the martyrdom of al-Ḥusain.
34. The poet means the 'Alid martyrs.
37. The reference is to the errors committed (from the Shī'ite standpoint) by

٢٨ عُمِّرَ منكم فى أذى تَفْضَحُكم   أخباره فى سِيَرِ الملاحم

٢٩ بين قتيلٍ منكمُ محارب   يكفر أو منافقٍ مسالم

٣٠ ثم قضى مسلَّمًا من ريبةٍ   فلم يكن من غدركم بسالم

٣١ نقضتمُ عهوده فى أهله   وحُلْتُمُ عن سَنَنِ المراسم

٣٢ وقد شهدتم مقتل ٱبن عمّه   خيرِ مُصلٍّ بعده وصائم

٣٣ وما استحلّ باغيا إمامُكُمْ   يزيدُ بالطفّ من ابن فاطم

٣٤ وها الى اليوم الظبا خاضبةٌ   من دمه مَناسرَ القشاعم

٣٥ والفُرْسُ لمّا علقوا بدينه   لم تنل العروةَ كفٌّ فاصم

٣٦ فمَنْ إذًا أَجْدَرُ أن يملكها   مَوْقوفةً على النعيم الدائم

٣٧ لا بدّ يومًا أن تُقالَ عثرةٌ   من سابقٍ أو هفوة من حازم

٣٨ لو هبّت الريحُ نسيمًا أبدًا   لم يُتَعوَّذْ من أذى السمائم

٣٩ أو أمنت حسناء طُولَ عمرها   عينًا لما احتاجت الى التمائم

٤٠ خُذْ يا حسودى بين جنبيك جوًى   يرمى إلى قلبك بالضرائم

٤١ وٱقنع فقد فتُّك غيرَ خاملٍ   بالصغر أن تقرع سنّ نادم

٤٢ لا زلت منحوسَ الجزاء قَلِقًا   بوادعٍ وسَهِراً لنائم

Abū Bakr and ʻUmar in allowing themselves to be nominated caliph to the exclusion of the prior claim of ʻAlī.

38. Envy and malice are always active to work against the ʻAlid cause.

42. Mihyar concludes with a flourish of double *ṭibāq*.

17 AL-MA'ARRĪ

1 Souls stretching out their necks towards the resurrection, and error standing upright in folly!

2 You refuse obstinately ever to do a good action, and (yet) you make ready for the day of forgiveness!

3 Be not deluded by a smile from a friend, for his thoughts are (all) hatred and guile,

4 And men, whether children or aged, (the latter) grow grey in error or (the former) grow up (in it).

5 You foolishly love your worldly life, but it never bestowed on you what you desired.

6 Ever since your carnal soul became lusty as a young camel, you amble and shamble along in error.

7 Though the sleep of mortals shall be long, for the sleepers there must surely be an awakening.

8 Your infatuation with the wench is a languishing and a sorrow; an occasional visit is no joy to the passionate lover.

9 Though the blackness of Saturn should dye your hands, and though Suhā should be an ear-drop in your ear,

10 There shall not deliver you from the accidents of the nights a surpassing radiance or a constant wealth,

11 Neither shall any power protect you from being carried into captivity, not though the darkness be a veil over you.

12 I perceive the onset of darkness to be ampler of wing, yet (even) its black and besetting crow dies.

13 What then is amiss with Aquila, that it does not fly therein, and with night's clinging Scorpio, that it does not crawl?

---

17 Sources: *Luzūm mā lam yalzam* (ed. Amīn 'Abd al-'Azīz, Cairo, 1333/1915), I, 69–70.
Ṭaha Ḥusain, *Sharḥ Luzūm mā lam yalzam* (Cairo, 1954?), I, 310–19.

Metre: *wāfir*.

1. Note the *ṭibāq*.
2. Note the *jinās*. *Ta'abbā* is abbreviated for *tata'abbā*.
5. Note the *jinās*.
7. Note the *jinās*.

١٧ ابو العلاء المعرّى

١ نفوسٌ للقيامة تشرئبُّ   وغَىٌّ فى البطالة متلئبُّ

٢ تأبَّى أن تجىء الخيرَ يومًا   وأنت ليوم غفرانٍ تئبُّ

٣ فلا يَغْرُرْك بِشْرٌ من صديقٍ   فإنّ ضميره إحْنٌ وخِبُّ

٤ وإنّ الناس طفلٌ أو كبيرٌ   يشيب على الغواية أو يشِبُّ

٥ تحبّ حياتك الدنيا سفاهاً   وما جادت عليك بما تُحِبُّ

٦ وإنّك منذ كون النفس عَنْساً   لَتُوضِعُ فى الضلالة أو تَخُبُّ

٧ وإن طال الرقادُ من البرايا   فإنّ الراقدين لهم مَهَبُّ

٨ غرامُك بالفتاة ضنىً وغمٌّ   وليس يَسُرُّ من يشتاق غِبُّ

٩ لو انّ سواد كيوانٍ خِضَابٌ   بكفّك والسُها فى الأُذن حِبُّ

١٠ لما نجّاك من غِيَرِ الليالى   سناءٌ فارعٌ وغِنىً مُرِبُّ

١١ وما يحميك عِزٌّ أن تُسَبَّى   ولو أنّ الظلامَ عليك سِبُّ

١٢ أرى جُنْح الدُّجَى أَوْفَى جناحًا   ومات غرابُه الجَوْنُ المُرِبُّ

١٣ فما للنسر ليس يطير فيه   وعقربُه المُضِبَّةُ لا تَدِبُّ

---

8. For *ḍanan* Amin reads *khanan*. By "the wench" the world is intended, which grants its favours only occasionally.

9. Sc. though you reach out to capture the stars.

10. Note the *jinās*.

12. Note the *jinās*. The meaning is that night passes away as surely as day.

13. Heaven is even more impotent than earth; at least the earth's eagles and scorpions can move.

14 Does day reveal the sun to the beholder, when the sun has already risen, and its rising is in mist?

15 Eloquence did not ward off death from Socrates, neither did any medicine protect Hippocrates against it.

16 When you behold me fallen on the brink (of death), let me be; every man that entertains hope is doomed to perish;

17 And do not scare away the bird then from me, neither let your hands moisten a parched lip.

18 IBN ZAIDŪN

1 Indeed I remembered you yearningly as you were in al-Zahrā', when the horizon was clear and the face of earth was shining,

2 And the breeze had a languor in its evening hours as if it had pity for me, and so languished out of compassion,

3 And the garden smiled, disclosing its silver water, as if you had loosened collars from the upper breasts.

4 A day like the days of pleasure for us now departed—we passed the night (like) thieves of that (pleasure), whilst fortune slept,

5 Diverting ourselves with eye-catching flowers, the dew running over them till they bent their necks,

6 As if their eyes, beholding my sleeplessness, wept for my condition, and the tears wandered glistening.

7 A rose shone in its sunburnt bed, and noonday glowed more intensely to the sight on account of it.

8 A nenuphar passed, redolent, embracing it, a slumberer whose eyes dawn had wakened.

9 Everything stirred in us a recollection making us long for you, a recollection which the breast was yet too constricted to hold.

---

17. Note the *jinās*. The poet refers to the Zoroastrian practice of exposing dead bodies to the carrion birds.

18 Sources: A. Cour, *Ibn Zaidoûn* (Constantine, 1920), 25 (textes).
Nuṣūṣ, 79.

Metre: *basīṭ*.

This poem was written for Ibn Zaidūn's beloved Wallāda.

١٤ أيجلو الشمسَ للرائى نهارٌ   فقد شرقت ومشرقُها مُضِبُّ

١٥ ولم يدفع ردى سقراطَ لفظٌ   ولا بقراط حامى عنه طِبُّ

١٦ اذا آنستَنى بشفاً صريعاً   فدعْنى كلُّ ذى أَمَلٍ يَتِبُّ

١٧ ولا تَذْبُبْ هناك الطير عنّى   ولا تَبْلُلْ يداك فماً يَذِبُّ

١٨ ابن زيدون

١ إنّى ذكرتُك بالزهراء مشتاقاً   والأفق طلقٌ ووجهُ الارض قد راقا

٢ وللنسيم ٱعتلال فى أصائله   كأنّما رقّ لى فٱعتلّ إشفاقا

٣ والروض عن مائه الفضّىّ مبتسمٌ   كما حللتَ عن اللّبات أطواقا

٤ يومٌ كأيّام لذّاتٍ لنا ٱنصرمت   بِتْنا لها حين نام الدهرُ سرّاقا

٥ نلهو بما يستميل العينَ من زَهَرٍ   جال الندى فيه حتّى مال أعناقا

٦ كأنّ أعينَه إذ عاينت أرقى   بكتْ لما بى فجال الدمعُ رقراقا

٧ وردٌ تألّق فى ضاحى منابته   فٱزداد منه الضحى فى العين إشراقا

٨ سرى ينافحه نيلوفرٌ عبقٌ   وسنانُ نبّه منه الصبح أحداقا

٩ كلٌّ يُهيج لنا ذكرى تشوّقنا   إليك لم يعدُ عنها الصدرُ أن ضاقا

---

1. "In al-Zahrā'": a fashionable quarter of Moorish Cordova.
2. Note the *jinās* (*al-ishtiqāq*).
3. The silver stream is compared with Wallāda's silvery throat.
4. Note the *ṭibāq* between *yaumun* and *bitnā*.
6. Note the *jinās* (*al-mushābih*).
7. Note the *jinās*.

10 If only death had fulfilled our union with you, it would have been the most generous of days.

11 May God not give rest to a heart visited by your remembrance, and it did not fly on the fluttering wings of yearning!

12 Had the zephyr's breath when it blew wished to transport me, it would have brought to you a youth emaciated by what he had encountered.

13 Not my most precious and prized possession, beloved of my soul —if lovers can be said to acquire possessions—

14 Would be fair recompense for the pure love in a time spent in the garden of intimacy, where we roved at will.

15 And now I praise God for the time we spent together, for which you have found consolation, whilst we have remained (true) lover.

19 IBN AL-KHAIYĀṬ

1 This pretty, twanging boy poured out for me with his eyes the like of (the wine) which was in his hands,

2 And I did not know which of the two it was that intoxicated me, and which of his two potions was the wine.

3 He appeared in a green gown of his, just like a graceful garden comprising blossoms,

4 And the pearl grieved because of his (glittering) teeth, and the anemone was put to shame by his cheeks.

5 Scarcely could I recover from my intoxication; and how should the passionate lover (ever) recover?

6 On my liver is the coolness of complaisance proceeding from him, even though in my heart is a fire proceeding from him.

7 And I am not the first man of ardent love who in (his) love was laden what he could not support.

---

19 Source: *Dīwān*, ed. Khalīl Mardam Beg (Damascus, 1377/1958), 220.
Metre: *mutaqārib*.

1. *shibha llatī*: the feminine relative is used because "wine" (understood) is feminine in Arabic. The adjective *l-aghannu* connotes "speaking with a twang as happens at puberty", see Lane 2299. Note the elegance of mentioning two parts of the body in the same verse, here heightened by both being in the dual.

١٠ لو كان وفّى المنا فى جمعنا بكم   لكان من أكرَم الأيّام أخلاقا

١١ لا سكّن اللّه قلباً عنّ ذكركُمُ   فلم يَطِرْ بجناح الشوق خَفّاقا

١٢ لو شاء حَمْلِى نسيمُ الريح حين هفا   وافاكُمُ بفتىً أضناه ما لاقى

١٣ لا علقى الأخْطَرَ الأسْنَى الحبيبِ إلى   نفسى إذا ما ٱقتنى الأحبابُ أعلاقا

١٤ كان التجازى بمحض الودّ من زمن   ميدان أنسٍ جرينا فيه إطلاقا

١٥ فالآن أَحْمَدُ ما كنّا لعهدكمُ   سلوتمُ وبقينا نحن عُشّاقا

١٩ ابن الخيّاط

١ سَقَانِي بِعَيْنَيْهِ شِبْهَ ٱلَّتِي   بِكَفَّيْهِ هَذَا ٱلْأَغَنُّ ٱلرَّشِيقُ

٢ فَلَمْ أَدْرِ أَيُّهُمَا ٱلْمُسْكِرِى   وَأَىُّ ٱلشَّرَابَيْنِ مِنْهُ ٱلرَّحِيقُ

٣ بَدَا فِى قَبَاءٍ لَهُ أَخْضَرٍ   كَمَا ضِمنَ ٱلنَّوْرَ رَوْضٌ أَنِيقُ

٤ وَقَدْ أَسِيَ ٱلدُّرُّ مِنْ ثَغْرِهِ   وَأُخْجِلَ مِنْ وَجْنَتَيْهِ ٱلشَّقِيقُ

٥ فَمَا كِدْتُ مِنْ سَكْرَتِي أَنْ أُفِيقَ   وَكَيْفَ يُفِيقُ ٱلْمُحِبُّ ٱلْمَشُوقُ

٦ عَلَى كَبِدِى مِنْهُ بَرْدُ ٱلرِّضَى   وَإِنْ كَانَ فِي ٱلْقَلْبِ مِنْهُ ٱلْحَرِيقُ

٧ وَلَسْتُ بِأَوَّلِ ذِى صَبْوَةٍ   تَحَمَّلَ فِى ٱلْحُبِّ مَا لَا يُطِيقُ

---

2. For the construction *l-muskirī*, see Wright, II, 65 A.
3. For the poetic use of the triptote inflection *akhḍarin*, see Wright, II, 387 B.
4. Note the *mulā'ama* between the two halves of this verse. There is elegance in the contrast between two colours.
6. Note the *ṭibāq* between *bardu* and *l-ḥarīqu*, and the elegant contrast between two parts of the body.

20 IBN KHAFĀJA

1 Oft-times a guest of a phantom of one who had deserted has approached, on whose account the complained-of one has passed the night the object of gratitude,

2 And beauty has cleared for him a way whereby the one blamed is received with his excuses accepted

3 And a hollow outspread, revealing a page in which beauty may be read inscribed.

4 He visited what time the wind of daybreak had tucked up the skirt of a cloud which had been trailed all night

5 And hung about the necks of those hills scattered pearls consisting of white blossoms,

6 And dawn had rent from his throat the buttoned-up collar of a darkness,

7 And the pitch blackness disclosed a brilliancy, and the musk converted to camphor

8 Where the muffled horsemen were driven away under the outspread banner of beauty.

9 Then he proceeded to envelop my heart in fire and to dazzle my eyes with light,

10 Just like the bough of the hillock bending pliantly, or the wild calf gazing startled.

11 The wine of passion had intoxicated his flank, so that he quivered intoxicated in his two cloaks

12 Behaving obstreperously, his gaze wounding me; yet the sin of drunkenness was pardonable.

13 He despatched a glance contracted out of delicacy, and took a short pace forward,

14 And the teardrops flowed upon his cheek, and the garden of beauty shone in the rain.

---

20 Source: *Dīwān* (ed. Muṣṭafā Ghāzī, Alexandria, 1960), 248.
Metre: *sarīʿ*.

1. The poet draws the conventional picture of a phantom visitation from the beloved who had deserted the lover, turning his complaints into expressions of gratitude. Note the *ṭibāq* and *jinās* (*lāḥiq* and *zā'id*).

2. Note the *ṭibāq* and *jinās* (*lāḥiq*).

3. One must suppose the lover to be sleeping (as often in such poems) on the margin of a stream, conventionally compared with a page on which the mirrored reflection of natural beauty constitutes the writing. Note the *jinās* (*mukhtalif*).

٢٠ ابن خفاجة

١ وضيفِ طيفٍ أمَّ من هاجرٍ بات به المشكوُّ مشكورا
٢ وقد جلا الحسنُ له سُنّةً يُلْقَى بها المعذولُ معذورا
٣ وصحفةً تُنْشَرُ من صفحةٍ يُقْرَأُ فيها الحسنُ مسطورا
٤ زار وريحُ الفجر قد قلّصتْ ذيل غمامٍ بات مجرورا
٥ وقلّدتْ أجيادَ تلك الربى درًّا من النُوّار منثورا
٦ والصبحُ قد مزّق عن نحره جيبَ ظلامٍ كان مزرورا
٧ فآنجابت الدهمة عن شهبةٍ وآلت المسكةُ كافورا
٨ بحيث خيلُ اللثم مطرودة تحت لواء الحسن منشورا
٩ ثم مضى يغشى به خاطرى نارًا ويعشى ناظرى نورا
١٠ كما آنثنى غصنُ النقَى أملدًا والتفت الجؤذرُ مذعورا
١١ قد أسكرتْ خمرُ الصبى عطفَه فماد فى بُرْدَيْه مخمورا
١٢ مُعَرْبِدًا يجرحنى طرفُه وكان ذنبُ السكر مغفورا
١٣ وأرسل اللحظةَ مكسورةً من تَرَفٍ والخطوَ مقصورا
١٤ وسال قطرُ الدمع فى خدّه فرفّ روضُ الحسن ممطورا

---

7. Note the double *ṭibāq*.
9. Note the *ṭibāq* and *jinās*.
10. The poet employs conventional images depicting young beauty.
11. Note the *jinās*.
12. The glance of the beloved is often compared with an arrow wounding the heart of the lover.
13. "Contracted": i.e. the lids being wrinkled. A boy is said to be *mutraf* when he is "made soft, or delicate, in body, and rendered submissive" (Lane 304, col. 2). Note the *jinās* (doubly *lāḥiq*).

21 IBN ZUHR

1 Resign the affair to destiny—that is more profitable to the soul—

2 And make the most of it when there advances the shining face of a full moon. Do not talk of cares, do not!—

3 Whatever is past and has come to an end cannot be brought back by sorrow—

4 And greet the morning with a cup of wine from the hand of a soft gazelle; when he parts (his lips) to disclose an ordered row (of pearly teeth)

5 Therein a lightning has flashed, and a wine a-glitter.

6 I will be the ransom for the fawn that he is, slender of stature and waist; he has been given beauty to drink, and has become intoxicated.

7 When he turns his back and goes away, then my heart is torn to pieces.

8 Who will succour a lover who was excited with desire, and was drowned in his tears when they set forth in the direction of the enclosure of al-'Aqīq

9 And they mounted at the place of the tamarisks? I cry alas for the day they said farewell.

10 What do you think? When the cavalcade set forth and rode at midnight, and the night was garmented in radiance,

11 Was it their light that shone forth, or was Joshua with the riders?

---

21 Sources: al-Maqqarī, *Nafḥ al-ṭīb* (Cairo, 1368/1949), III, 19–20.
A. R. Nykl, *Hispano-Arabic Poetry* (Baltimore, 1946), 250–1.

Metre: *khafīf*.

This popular song is a *muwashshaḥa* with the pattern A B a a a A B b b b A B c c c A B d d d A B e e e A B.

2. The full moon is the conventional image for the face of a beautiful boy or girl. Note the implicit *ṭibāq* between *badrin* and *tahallala*.

4. The "daughter of the vine" is of course wine. The youthful saki is often compared with a gazelle.

5. The lightning is the flashing teeth, the wine is the saliva gleaming on the teeth, both conventional images.

٢١ ابن زهر

١ سَلِّمِ الأمر للقَضا فهو للنفس أنْفَعُ

٢ وٱغْتَنِمْ حين اقبلا وجهُ بدرٍ تهلّلا لا تَقُلْ بالهموم لا

٣ كلّ ما فات وٱنقضى ليس بالحزن يُرجَعُ

٤ وٱصْطَبِحْ بٱبنة الكروم من يدى شادنٍ رخيم حين يفترّ عن نظيم

٥ فيه برقٌ قد أومَضا ورحيقٌ مُشَعْشَعُ

٦ أنا أفديه من رشا أهْيَفِ القدّ والحشا سُقِيَ الحُسْنَ فٱنتشى

٧ مذ تولّى وأعرضا ففؤادى يُقَطَّعُ

٨ مَنْ لصبٍّ غدا مَشُوق ظلّ فى دمعه غريق حين أمّوا حِمَى العقيق

٩ واستقلّوا بذى الغضا أسفى يوم ودّعوا

١٠ ما ترى حين أظعنا وسرى الركب مَوْهِنا واكتسى الليل بالسنا

١١ نورُهم ذا الذى أضا أم مع الركب يُوشَعُ

---

6. "Intoxicated": with the pride of youthful beauty.

8. "The enclosure of al-'Aqīq": a location near Medina, see Yāqūt, IV, 199, and cf. my *The Mystical Poems of Ibn al-Fāriḍ*, 97.

9. "The place of the tamarisks": see *The Mystical Poems*, *ibid.* The topographical references are conventional.

10. The reference is to Joshua halting the sun from setting; Nykl missed this point, and his translation is therefore sadly astray. Ibn Zuhr here quotes from Abū Tammām:

fa-wa-llāhi mā adrī a-aḥlāmu nā'imin
alammat bi-nā am kāna fi l-rakbi yūsha'u.

22 IBN ʿUNAIN

1 Ask the backs of the horses on the day of battle concerning us, if our signs are unknown, and the limber lances

2 On the morning we met before Damietta a mighty host of Byzantines, not to be numbered either for certain or (even) by guesswork.

3 They agreed as to opinion and resolution and ambition and religion, even if they differed in language.

4 They called upon their fellow-Crusaders, and troops (of them) advanced as though the waves were ships for them,

5 Upon them every manner of mailcoat of armour, glittering like the horn of the sun, firmly woven together.

6 A delusion made them eager to (try conclusions with) us, and they galloped at us swiftly on fleet steeds, and we galloped,

7 And the tawny lances ceased not thrusting at them with their edges till they sought protection of us against us.

8 We gave them to drink a cup which banished slumber from them; and how shall a man sleep through the night when he is deprived of security?

9 They endured right handsomely, and resisted a long time; but resistance was vain and availed not.

10 They met death from the blue lance-points, red, and surrendered to us, and we treated (them) well.

11 Well-doing has ever been a characteristic of ours, which sons have inherited in turn from noble fathers.

12 We bestowed on them that remained a new life, so that they lived with necks invested with necklaces of favour;

13 And had they prevailed, they would not have failed to lap our blood; but we prevailed, and we acted with forbearance.

---

22 Source: *Dīwān* (ed. Khalīl Mardam Beg, Damascus, 1365/1946), 29–32.
Metre: *ṭawīl*.
This poem was composed to celebrate the victory of Damietta in 618/1221, in which the Aiyūbid al-Malik al-Kāmil utterly defeated a three-years' Crusade and recaptured the town and stronghold. See *Encycl. of Isl.*[2], II, 292; P. Hitti, *History of the Arabs*, 653–4.

1. The editor tentatively proposes to emend *āyātunā* to *ābā'unā* ("our fathers").

٢٢ ابن عنين

١ سلوا صَهَوَات الخيل يوم الوغى عنّا   اذا جُهلت آياتُنا والقنا اللُدْنا

٢ غداةَ لقينا دون دِمْيَاطَ جحفلاً   من الروم لا يُحْصَى يقيناً ولا ظنّا

٣ قد اتّفقوا رأياً وعزماً وهمّةً   وديناً وإن كانوا قد اختلفوا لُسْنا

٤ تداعوا بأنصار الصليب فأقبلت   جموعٌ كأنّ الموج كان لهم سُفْنا

٥ عليهم من الماذيّ كلُّ مُفَاضَةٍ   دِلاصٍ كقرن الشمس قد أحكمت وَضْنا

٦ وأطمعهم فينا غرورٌ فأرقلوا   إلينا سراعًا بالجياد وأرقلنا

٧ فما برحت سمرُ الرماح تنوشهم   بأطرافها حتّى استجاروا بنا مِنّا

٨ سقيناهمُ كأسًا نفتْ عنهمُ الكرى   وكيف ينام الليلَ مَنْ عَدِمَ الأَمْنا

٩ لقد صبروا صبراً جميلا ودافعوا   طويلًا فما أَجْدَى دفاعٌ ولا أَغْنَى

١٠ لقوا الموت من زُرْق الأسنّة أحمراً   فألقوا بأيديهم إلينا فأَحْسَنَّا

١١ وما برح الإحسانُ منّا سجيّةً   توارثها عن صِيد آبائنا الأَبْنَا

١٢ منحنا بقاياهم حياةً جديدةً   فعاشوا بأعناقٍ مقلَّدةٍ مَنَّا

١٣ ولو ملكوا لم يأتلوا فى دمائنا   ولوغًا ولكنّا ملكنا فأَسْجَحْنَا

---

3. Note the *ṭibāq* in this graphic description of the multilingual forces of the Crusaders.

5. "Horn of the sun": its upper part, or its first rays on rising, see Freytag, III, 435*a*.

7. "Of us against us": they threw themselves upon our mercy.

9. "Right handsomely": a cliché from Koran, XII, 18, 83.

12. *Mannan*: accus. of *tamyīz*, i.e. "they owed their lives to us".

14 They had proved us before that in engagements, in which the inexperienced ones of our people learned how to thrust;

15 How many a monarch (there was) whose straps we bound, and how many a captive we freed from the misery of captivity!

16 Lions of the fray—but for the smiting of our swords they would never have worn chains or dwelt in prison.

17 And how many a day of heat (there has been) whose noontide we have not countered with any covering, and of bitter cold against which we have not sought any shelter!

18 The comfort of a king is procured in the rigour of hardship, and the sweetness of glory is gathered from bitterness.

19 We are led by a noble scion of the House of Aiyūb, whose resolution disdains to be settled in any place of contentment,

20 Noble in praise, devoid of shame, valorous, handsome of countenance, perfect in beauty and beneficence.

21 By your life, the signal deeds of 'Īsā are not hidden, they shine out radiant as the sun upon the farthest as the nearest.

22 He marched towards Damietta with every highborn champion, viewing the descent into battle as the most salubrious of descents,

23 And he removed therefrom the miscreants of Byzantium, and the hearts of certain men were gladdened that afterwards made compact with sorrow;

24 And he cleansed her of their impurity with his sword—a hero regarding the acquisition of praise as the noblest of prizes.

25 His swords have immortalised the memorable deeds of glory, whose report will never pass away, though time itself shall perish.

26 Our swords and their necks have known their places of encounter there; and if they return to the attack, we too shall return!

---

15. Note the *jinās* and *ṭibāq*.
16. "Lions of the fray": qualifying "how many a monarch".
17. Note the *ṭibāq*, *mulā'ama* and internal rhyme.
18. Note the double *ṭibāq*.
19. The reference is to al-Malik al-Kāmil, grandson of Aiyūb the founder of the Aiyūbid dynasty.

١٤ وقد جرّبونا قبلها فى وقائعٍ   تعلّم غُمر القوم منّا بها الطعنا

١٥ فكم من مليكٍ قد شددنا إساره   وكم من أسيرٍ من شقا الأسْر أطْلَقنا

١٦ أُسُودُ وغىً لولا قراعُ سيوفنا   لما ركبوا قيدًا ولا سكنوا سِجْنَا

١٧ وكم يوم حرٍّ ما لقينا هجيرَه   بسترٍ وقُرٍّ ما طلبنا له كِنَّا

١٨ فإنّ نعيم الملك فى شظَف الشقا   يُنال وحلوَ العزّ من مُرّةٍ يُجْتَنَى

١٩ يسيرُ بنا من آل أيّوبَ ماجدٌ   أبى عزمُه أن يستقرّ به مغنى

٢٠ كريمُ الثنا عارٍ من العار باسلٌ   جميلُ المحيّا كاملُ الحسن والحسنى

٢١ لعمرُك ما آيات عيسى خفيّةٌ   هى الشمس للأقصى سناءً وللأدنى

٢٢ سرى نحو دمياطٍ بكلّ سمَيْذَعٍ   نجيبٍ يرى وِرْدَ الوغى الموردَ الأهْنَا

٢٣ فأجْلَى علوجَ الروم عنها وأفْرِحَتْ   قلوبُ رجالٍ حالفتْ بعدها الحزنا

٢٤ وطهّرها من رجسهم بحسامه   همامٌ يرى كسب الثنا المغنم الأسنى

٢٥ مآثرُ مجدٍ خلّدتها سيوفه   لها نبأ يفنى الزمانُ ولا يفنى

٢٦ وقد عرفت أسيافُنا ورقابُهم   مواقعَها فيها فإن عاودوا عُدْنا

---

20. Note the *jinās* (*mushābih*) and the punning use of *kamilu*.
21. ʿĪsā: al-Malik al-Kāmil's brother (d. 624/1227).
22. "The descent": the familiar image of coming down to water.
23. "Certain men": the Christians.

23 IBN AL-FĀRIḌ

1 We drank upon the remembrance of the Beloved a wine wherewith we were drunken before ever the vine was created.

2 The full moon was a cup for it, itself being the sun that a crescent moon passes round; and how many a star shows forth when it is mingled!

3 And but for its fragrance, I would never have been guided to its tavern; and but for its radiance, the imagination would never have pictured it;

4 And Time has left naught of it but a last gasp, as if its vanishing were a concealment in the breasts of (human) reasons.

5 Yet if it is (merely) mentioned in the tribe, the tribesmen become intoxicated, and there is no shame nor guilt upon them.

6 From amidst the bowels of the vats it has mounted up, and nothing remains of it in truth but a name;

7 Yet if upon a day it comes into the thoughts of a man, manifold joy will dwell in him, and sorrow will depart.

8 And had the boon-companions seen (merely) the seal-impress upon its vessel, that impress would have intoxicated them, without (the wine) itself;

9 And had they sprinkled therewith the dust of a dead man's tomb, the spirit would have returned to him and his body would have been quickened.

10 And had they cast, in the shadow of the wall of its vine, a sick man already nigh to death, the sickness would have departed from him;

11 And had they brought nigh its tavern one paralysed, he would have walked; and the dumb would have spoken at the (mere) mention of its flavour;

---

23 Sources: *Dīwān* (Marseilles, 1853), 472–500.
A. J. Arberry, *The Mystical Poems of Ibn al-Fāriḍ*, 81–90.

Metre: *ṭawīl*.

For other translations of this celebrated poem see R. A. Nicholson, *Studies in Islamic Mysticism* (Cambridge, 1921), 184–8 (excellently annotated); E. Dermenghem, *Al-Khamriya* (Paris, 1931). Many Arab authors wrote commentaries on this poem; the most authoritative was the Syrian mystic 'Abd al-Ghanī al-Nābulusī (d. 1143/1730).

The following paraphrase will help to explain the elaborate mystical symbolism. The poet opens by making an unambiguous "reprobate's confession": he and

٢٣ ابن الفارض

١ شربنا على ذكر الحبيب مدامةً   سكرنا بها من قبل أن يُخْلَق الكرم

٢ لها البدر كأس وهى شمس يديرها   هلال وكم يبدو إذا مزِجَت نجم

٣ ولولا شذاها ما اهتديتُ لحانها   ولولا سناها ما تصوّرها الوهم

٤ ولم يُبْقِ منها الدهرُ غير حشاشة   كأنّ خفاها فى صدور النُهى كتم

٥ فإن ذُكرت فى الحىّ أصبح أهله   نشاوَى ولا عارٌ عليهم ولا إثم

٦ ومن بين أحشاء الدنان تصاعدت   ولم يَبْقَ منها فى الحقيقة إلاّ آسم

٧ وإن خطرت يومًا على خاطر آمرئٍ   أقامت به الأفراحُ وارتحل الهمّ

٨ ولو نظر الندمان ختم إنائها   لأسكرهم من دونها ذلك الختم

٩ ولو نضحوا منها ثرى قبر ميّتٍ   لعادت اليه الروح وانتعش الجسم

١٠ ولو طرحوا فى فىء حائط كرمها   عليلا وقد أشفى لفارقه السقم

١١ ولو قرّبوا من حانها مُقْعَدًا مشى   وينطق من ذكرى مذاقتها البكم

---

his companions in the mystical circle have drunk wine at the mention of the Beloved's name—but it is a Wine with which they were intoxicated before ever the Vine was created (line 1), this Vine being, as we have suggested for us later (line 30), the physical universe. What is the Wine then? Surely the source of holy rapture, the Love of God manifested in His creation and indwelling in the human soul. The Moon, symbol of the radiant Spirit of Muḥammad, is the cup in which that sun-like Wine is contained; this cup of esoteric knowledge is passed round the circle of Muslim mystics by the "new moon", whose crescent shape is perhaps intended to suggest the Elder bent by long devotions; the lights of spiritual illumination,

12 And had the breaths of its perfume been wafted through the East, and in the West were one whose nostrils were stopped, smell would have returned to him;

13 And had the hand of one touching it been henna'd from the cup of it, he would not have strayed in any night, having in his hand the star;

14 And had it been secretly unveiled to one blind, he would have become endowed with sight; and the deaf would hear at the sound of its filtering;

15 And had a cavalcade set forth seeking the soil of its native land, and amidst the cavalcade one stung by a snake, the poison would not have harmed him;

16 And had an enchanter drawn the letters of its name upon the forehead of one stricken with madness, the inscription would have cured him;

17 And had its name been inscribed above the banner of an army, that superscription would have intoxicated all beneath the banner.

18 It amends the manners of the boon-campanions, so that he who was irresolute is guided by it to the path of firm resolve,

19 And he whose hand knew not munificence (suddenly) becomes generous, and he who had no forbearance is clement in time of rage.

20 And the fool of the tribe, had his lips attained to kiss its filter, that kiss would have endowed him with the essence of its fine qualities.

21 They say to me, "Describe it, for you are well-informed of its description". Indeed, I have some knowledge of its attributes:

22 Purity, yet no water, and subtility, yet no air, and light, yet no fire, and spirit, yet no body.

---

kindled by the fervour of the Wine mingling with the mystics' souls, twinkle like stars in a darkened firmament (line 2).

Once the Wine was all-pervading, but now its glory is greatly dimmed; only its fragrance and unimaginable lustre have guided the poet's footsteps to the inn where it may still be found, the inner circle of the Sufi mysteries (line 3), for all that is left of it in these latter days is as it were a last gasp, hidden deep in the breasts of the faithful few (line 4). Indeed, it has wholly vanished but for its name; yet the mention of its name alone suffices to intoxicate the innocent mystic (lines 5–6). The very thought of the Wine brings great joy and drives away sorrow (line 7); the observation of its effect upon the saints is enough to transport the neophyte (line 8).

١٢ ولو عبقت فى الشرق أنفاس طيبها   وفى الغرب مزكومٌ لعاد له الشمّ

١٣ ولو خُضبت من كأسها كفُّ لامسٍ   لما ضلّ فى ليل وفى يده النجم

١٤ ولو جُلِيَتْ سرًّا على أكمهٍ غدا   بصيراً ومن راووقها تسمع الصمّ

١٥ ولو أنّ ركباً يمّموا ترب أرضها   وفى الركب ملسوعٌ لما ضرّه السمّ

١٦ ولو رسم الراقى حروف ٱسمها على   جبينِ مُصابٍ جُنَّ أبرأه الرسم

١٧ وفوق لواء الجيش لو رُقِمَ ٱسمها   لأسكر من تحت اللوا ذلك الرقم

١٨ تهذّب أخلاقَ الندامى فيهتدى   بها لطريق العزم من لا له عزم

١٩ ويكرم من لم يعرف الجودَ كفُّه   ويحلم عند الغيظ من لا له حلم

٢٠ ولو نال فدم القوم لثم فدامه   لأكسبه معنى شمائلها اللثم

٢١ يقولون لى صِفْها فأنت بوصفها   خبيرٌ أَجَلْ عندى بأوصافها علم

٢٢ صفاءٌ ولا ماءٌ ولطفٌ ولا هوًا   ونورٌ ولا نارٌ وروحٌ ولا جسم

The Wine's powers, had they been put to the test, would have proved truly miraculous, bringing the dead to life, healing the sick, making the paralysed to walk and the dumb to speak, unstopping the stopped-up nostrils, giving light to those in darkness, restoring sight to the blind and hearing to the deaf, rendering harmless the snake's venomous bite, mending the mind deranged, spurring warriors to superhuman valour, endowing all amiable qualities, strengthening the resolve of the irresolute, converting the fool to prudence (lines 9–20).

The attributes of this Wine are those of the four elements themselves, but without their gross materiality (lines 21–2). It inspires matchless eloquence, and moves the heart to infinite gladness (lines 23–4 in Arberry, 31–2 in other editions). It existed

23 The tale of it told in eternity was more ancient than all existing things, when neither shape nor trace was there;

24 And through it all things subsisted there for a purpose wise, whereby it was veiled from every man not having understanding.

25 And my spirit was distraught for it, so that the twain were mingled in unification, and not as a body is permeated by another;

26 So (there is) a wine without a vine, when Adam is (reckoned) a father to me, and a vine without a wine, when its "mother" is (reckoned) my mother.

27 Now, the subtility of the vessels is really consequential upon the subtility of the inward truths, and the inward truths augment by means of the vessels;

28 And the division (truly) has occurred, whilst (yet) the whole is one, our spirits being the wine and our corporeal shapes the vine.

29 Before it is no "before", and no "after" is after it; and as for the priority of (all) posterities, that is the Wine's for a surety.

30 Ere Time's term was straitened, then was its pressing-time; after the Wine was our father's epoch, itself being orphan.

31 (These are) beauties, which guide its describers aright to appraise it, so that in prose and verse they tell of it in beauteous words,

32 And he who knew it not rejoices when it is mentioned, as Nu'm's yearning lover whenever Nu'm is named.

33 Then they said, "You have imbibed sin". No indeed, but I imbibed that which, in my opinion, it would be sin (itself) to eschew.

34 Good health to the folk of the monastery! How oft they were drunken with it, yet they never (truly) imbibed it but (only) aspired to do so.

35 But I—I was set awhirl with it, before ever I grew (to manhood), and with me that rapture shall abide forever, though my bones may crumble.

---

before Time began, and through it all living things subsisted from the beginning in a unification of spirit with Spirit (lines 25(23)–27(25)). The fatherhood of Adam relates only to the carnal soul; the immortal spirit is the child of the Vine, being an epiphany of the Love of God (line 28(26)). This spirit informs the body with its own ethereality, while the body extends the spirit's dominion over the material world, the Vine in which the Wine is perpetually renewed; but the Wine itself exists from all eternity, being the seal set before creation upon all succeeding ages (lines 29(27)–32(30)).

To drink that Wine is no sin, as some allege; rather is it the unforgivable sin not to taste of it (line 33). The Christians, though never having drunk of this Wine, knew

٢٣	تقدّم كلّ الكائنات حديثُها	قديمًا ولا شكلٌ هناك ولا رسم
٢٤	وقامت بها الأشياء ثَمّ لحكمةٍ	بها احتجبت عن كلّ من لا له فهم
٢٥	وهامت بها روحى بحيث تمازجا اتّ	حادًا ولا جرمٌ تخلّله جرم
٢٦	فخمرٌ ولا كرمٌ وآدم لى أبٌ	وكرمٌ ولا خمرٌ ولى أمّها أمّ
٢٧	ولطفُ الأوانى فى الحقيقة تابعٌ	للطف المعانى والمعانى بها تنمو
٢٨	وقد وقع التفريقُ والكلّ واحدٌ	فأرواحنا خمرٌ وأشباحنا كرم
٢٩	ولا قبلها قبلٌ ولا بعدَ بعدها	وقبليّة الأبعاد فهى لها حتم
٣٠	وعصر المدى من قبله كان عصرها	وعهد أبينا بعدها ولها اليتم
٣١	محاسنُ تهدى المادحين لوصفها	فيحسن فيها منهمُ النثر والنظم
٣٢	ويطرب من لم يَدْرِها عند ذكرها	كمشتاق نُعْمٍ كلّما ذُكرت نعم
٣٣	وقالوا شربتَ الإثم كلّا وإنّما	شربتُ التى فى تركها عندى الإثم
٣٤	هنيئاً لأهل الدير كم سكروا بها	وما شربوا منها ولكنّهم همّوا
٣٥	وعندىَ منها نشوةٌ قبل نشأتى	معى أبدًا تبقى وإن بَلِىَ العظم

of it, and therefore experienced some part of its intoxication (line 34); the poet himself being a Muslim born, has always been and will always be enraptured by it (line 35). He charges his hearer to drink it pure; or if mingled, then only watered with the gleaming moisture of the Beloved's mouth, the teachings of the Prophet (line 36). It is to be found in the mystic circle, to the accompaniment of music (line 37); it drives out all sorrow, and accords the mystic partaking of it a sense of transcending Time even for the brief space of his holy rapture (lines 38–9).

Not to drink of this Wine is to miss all the true gladness and wisdom of life; he that refuses to be a mystic may well weep for himself and his wasted sum of days (lines 40–1).

36 I charge you to take it pure; yet if you desire to mingle it, to turn away from the Beloved's mouth's lustre—that were wrong indeed.

37 So look for it in the tavern, and seek to unveil it there to the notes of melodies, wherewith it is a noble prize.

38 For never did it dwell with sullen care in the selfsame place, just as sorrow has never cohabited with sweet tunefulness.

39 And be your intoxication therewith but for the life of an hour, yet you shall see Time's self become an obedient slave, yours being the command (of it).

40 No joy is there in this world for him who lives sober; and he who dies not of drunkenness misses (true) prudence—

41 Then let him weep for himself, whose life is all wasted, he having neither part nor portion of the Wine.

24 BAHĀ' AL-DĪN ZUHAIR

1 Every thing from you is accepted (gratefully) and laid upon the eyes,

2 And what pleases you of my destruction is easy for me (to bear) and (readily) bestowed.

3 Fear not (to have committed) any sin or crime; the blood of lovers may be shed with impunity,

4 And for all the harshness that is in you, you are (still) to be trusted, and (still) the object of hope.

5 Alas for a passionate one concerning whom, in loving you, many stories have been told!

6 Amazing is my affliction—I am (at once) excusable and reproached.

7 I have a beloved whose name I do not divulge, of whom I am today slain;

8 He who owns me—in his character is weariness; I am (both) slave, and wearied of.

9 So till how long, O you who possess me, is every promise of yours postponed?

10 When I shall die of thirst, may the Nile not flow after me!

---

24 Sources: E. H. Palmer, *The Poetical Works of Behá-ed-Dín Zoheir* (Cambridge, 1876), I, 195.
Dīwān (Cairo, n.d.), 162.

Metre: *madīd.*

٣٦ عليك بها صرفًا وإن شئت مزجها   فعَدْلُك عن ظَلْم الحبيب هو الظُّلم

٣٧ فدونكها فى الحان وٱستَجْلِها به   على نغم الألحان فهى بها غنم

٣٨ فما سكنت والهمَّ يومًا بموضع   كذلك لم يسكن مع النَّغَم الغمّ

٣٩ وفى سكرة منها ولو عُمْرَ ساعةٍ   ترى الدهر عبدًا طائعًا ولك الحكم

٤٠ فلا عَيْشَ فى الدنيا لمن عاش صاحيًا   ومن لم يمت سكرًا بها فاته الحزم

٤١ على نفسه فَلْيَبكِ من ضاع عُمْرُهُ   وليس له فيها نصيب ولا سهم

٢٤ بهاء الدين زهير

١ كلّ شىء منك مقبول   وعلى العينَيْن محمول

٢ والذى يرضيك من تلفى   هَيِّنٌ عندى ومبذول

٣ لا تخفْ إثماً ولا حرجاً   فدمُ العشّاق مطلول

٤ وعلى ما فيك من صلَفٍ   أنت مأمونٌ ومأمول

٥ وَيْحَ صبٍّ فى محبّتكم   كثرت فيه الأقاويل

٦ وعجيبٌ ما بليت به   أنا معذورٌ ومعذول

٧ لى حبيبٌ لا أبوح به   أنا منه اليوم مقتول

٨ مالكى فى خلقه ملَلٌ   أنا مملوكٌ ومملول

٩ فإلى كم أنت يا ساكنى   كل وعد منك ممطول

١٠ واذا ما متّ من ظمأٍ   لا جرى من بعدى النيل

In this delicate little poem almost every couplet exhibits some variety of *jinās* or other rhetorical figure.

5. For the construction with *waiḥa*, see Wright, I, 296 A.

9. For *sākinī* Palmer reads *sakanī* ("my repose").

25 IBN SAHL

1 The earth had put on a green robe, whilst the dew was scattering pearls on its slopes;

2 It stirred (in the breeze), and I supposed the flowers were camphor there, and I thought the soil there was pungent musk,

3 And it was as though earth's lilies were embracing her roses—mouth kissing red cheek.

4 And the river between the meadows—you would suppose it to be a sword suspended in a green harness;

5 And the slopes ran along their side, so that I supposed them to be a hand tracing lines on the page.

6 And it was as though, when the pure silver (of the river) gleamed, the hand of the sun turned it into yellow gold.

7 And the birds—the preachers of them were standing there, having taken for a pulpit naught other than the arak-tree.

26 IBN ZĀKŪR

1 Pass round the cups of the wine of the lips' deep red—what a wine it is, rivalling the pomegranate-blossom!—

2 And pour it out to me as a wine clearing the soul; haply I shall find ease from the fever of (my) thirst.

---

25 Sources: *Dīwān* (Cairo, 1346/1928), 29–30.
Muntakhab, I, 196–7.

Metre: *kāmil.*

The images used in this charming little poem are the usual fancies employed by the Andalusian poets, as exemplified and annotated in the poem of Ibn Khafāja reproduced earlier.

2. For *at-turba* the reading *at-tibra* is given in *Dīwān*, obviously a misprint. Note the *ṭibāq* between *kāfūr* and *misk*.

3. Note the elegance of the pair of similes. *Thaghr* can mean both "mouth" and "front-teeth"—the latter lily-white in contrast with the rosy-red cheek.

4. The poet elaborates cleverly the stock comparison of a river with a sword, as for instance Ibn Shuhaid (d. 1034):

The sword is a sheathed rivulet, to whose brink
Death comes to drink,
The lance a bough, that drips a crimson flood
And fruits in blood.

٢٥   ابن سهل

١   الأرضُ قد لبستْ رداءً أَخْـضَـرَا   والطَّلُّ يَنْـشُرُ فى رُبـاها جوهـرا

٢   هـاجت فخلْتُ الزَّهْرَ كافورًا بها   وحسبتُ فيها التُّرْبَ مِسْكاً أذفـرا

٣   وكأنّ سوسنها يُـصَـافِـحُ وَرْدَهـا   ثَغْرٌ يُقَبِّلُ مـنـه خدًّا أحمـرا

٤   والنهرُ ما بيـن الرياض تـخالـه   سيفاً تَعَلَّقَ فى نِجَادٍ أخـضـرا

٥   وجرتْ بصفحتها الرُّبا فحسبتُـهـا   كفًّا يُنَمِّقُ فى الصحيفة أسطرا

٦   وكـأنّـه اذ لاح نـاصِعُ فِضَّـهٍ   جعلتْـه كفُّ الشمس تِبْراً أصفرا

٧   والطيرُ قد قامت بـه خُـطَبَاؤه   لم تَتَّخذ إلّا الاراكـةَ مـنبرا

٢٦   ابن زاكور

١   أَدِر الكأْسات من خمر اللَّعَسْ   يا لَها من راحْ   تحكى الجُلَّنـار

٢   وأَسـقـنـيـهـا خمرةً تجلو النَّفَسْ   عَـلَّـنـى أرتاح   من حـرّ الأُوار

5. For a similar image, compare Ibn Sa'īd (d. 1280):

> The river is a page
> Of parchment white;
> The breeze, that author sage,
> There loves to write.

> And when the magic screed
> Is finished fair,
> The bough leans down, to read
> His message there.

6. Note the *ṭibāq* between *fiḍḍatin* amd *tibran*.

26 Source: Abdul-lah Gannun el Hasani, *Poemas Selectos de Ibn Zakur* (Larache, 1942), 90–1.
Metre: based upon *ramal*.
This *muwashshaḥa* is constructed upon the scheme A B C A B C a b c a b c a b c
A B C A B C d e f d e f d e f A B C A B C. The images are all variants of the
conventional figures of Andalusian love-poetry.

3 With my father (I would ransom) a fawn that shot me with arrows whose feathers are eyelashes, transpiercing hearts.

4 He rent the sorrowful and bewildered heart when he gazed, and there was drawn a sword he made naked.

5 Ambergris-dark of mole, musky of last portion, baffling the mind the pearls which he arranged.

6 I was distraught with passion for his radiance, borrowed from the light of dawning, or from a shining full moon.

7 When a mouth parted, there shone like a brand one very bright and clear that kindled a fire-stick of a fire,

8 Narcissus-like of eye, rosy of cheeks, with the blood of livers shaming the anemone,

9 A moon of beauty over a bough of silver bending pliant, blood-brother to the ban-tree.

10 He drew against me the sword of (his) eyes, disabling the fore-arms, and the furnace grew fiercer.

11 My patience was exhausted in desire for a human fawn, and reason departed when the place of visitation withdrew afar,

12 And a shower of tears burst from my eyes, and passion was exposing that no veil could conceal.

27 AL-SHIDYĀQ

1 In the West hath arisen a light, (Oh! how bright a light!) which dispels all darkness from every quarter of the East:

2 It hath shone forth in a victorious region, over which reigns one who is VICTORIA in name as well as in deeds;

3 One possessed of distinctions to which no other mortal has attained, and glory of a prosperous reign which no glory can excel;

---

5. "Musky of last portion": from Koran, LXXXIII, 26.

27 Source: A. J. Arberry, "Fresh Light on Ahmad Faris al-Shidyaq", in *Islamic Culture*, XXVI (1952), 155–64.

Metre: *basīṭ*.

This panegyric to Queen Victoria was composed in 1850. The translation here printed is that made by al-Shidyāq himself and published privately as a broadsheet.

٣ بأبى ظَبْىٌ رمانى بسِهام   ريشُها الأهداب   تبرى الأفئدَه

٤ مزّق القلب الكئيب المستهام   إذ رنا وانساب   سيفٌ جرّدَه

٥ عنبرىُّ الخال مسكىّ الخِتام   يُذهل الألباب   درٌّ نضّدَه

٦ هِمْتُ وجدًا من سناه المقتبَسْ   من سنا الإصباح   أو بدرٍ أنار

٧ لاح حين افترّ ثغرٌ كالقَبَسْ   أزهرٌ وضّاح   أذكى زند نار

٨ نرجسىُّ اللحظ وردى الوجنتين   بدم الأكباد   أزرت بالشقيق

٩ بدرُ حسنٍ فوق غصنٍ من لُجَيْن   مائلٍ ميّاد   للبان شقيق

١٠ قد نضا نحوىَ سيف المقلتين   أوهن الأعضاد   واشتدّ الحريق

١١ عيل صبرى فى هوى ظبى الأَنَس   والحِجا قد راح   مذ شطّ المزار

١٢ ورذاذُ الدمع من عينى انبجس   والهوى فضّاح   لايُخفِى استتار

٢٧ الشدياق

١ فى الغرب مطلعُ نورٍ أيّما نور   يجلو عن الشرق طرًّا كلّ ديجور

٢ قد لاح فى أفقٍ فيه مليكته   منصورة الإسم والأفعال منصور

٣ ذاتُ المعالى التى ما حازها بَشَرٌ   وفخرُ ملكٍ سعيدٍ غير مفخور

Certain adjustments in the order of the lines of the translation have been made, to secure uniformity with the original poem. The *qaṣīda* abounds in rhetorical figures and is a very interesting early example of the nineteenth-century revival of the classical norms.

1. Note the double *ṭibāq*.
2. Note the *jinās*, and the punning use of *manṣūratun*.
3. Note the *jinās* and *mulā'ama*.

4 In whose days the world exults, so that none is to be found there, but those who are grateful and covered with Her favours.

5 In each remote province She has those who thank Her, though others find no praise even at home.

6 Her high renown indicates Her personal excellencies, as Her noble features reveal Her illustrious birth;

7 So that those who comprehend Her excellencies even from afar, may extol them fully as much as those who are near;

8 And he who is blest with the advantage of being near Her courts becomes indeed possessed of the highest felicity.

9 She seems mortal only in respect of Her sovereign power, for in Her perfections She is like one of the Houris;

10 God has given Her excellence of disposition and beauty of form, and exhibited Her in the fairest of shapes,

11 And chosen Her to a dignity for which none other is fit, and which is altogether unequalled and incomparable.

12 Through Her the rest of Her sex have been exalted to an elevation so glorious as to excel the rest of creation;

13 Nor shall men henceforth have any rank, or fame, or precedence above women.

14 So noble is She in descent and actions, that Her praise is due as an obligatory peace-offering, to be paid by every tongue.

15 If mortals were not created to be inhabitants of this lower world, She would have ever dwelt in the unseen region of the heavens;

16 And if man's virtues could make him immortal, She would have been the first to be destined to immortality.

17 God has given Her Her desires as if at Her absolute will and pleasure.

18 Blessed is the region in which Her presence is revealed! For it is thereby adorned with every thing that can cheer.

19 If the sunshine often leaves it, it is from shame, for Her countenance is more brilliant than the light.

---

6. Note the *jinās* and *ṭibāq*.
7. Note the *jinās* and *ṭibāq*.
10. Note the *jinās*.
12. Note the triple *jinās*.

٤ زَهَتْ بأيّامها الدنيا فلست ترى   بـهـا سِوى شـاكـرٍ بالنّيل مغمور

٥ فى كلّ قطرٍ من الأقطار شاكرها   إذ غـيـرهـا فى حماه غير مشكور

٦ دلّتْ عـلـى ذاتها كُبْرَى مآثرها   كـمـا خـفـا سَرْوَها سِرُّ الأسارير

٧ فمَنْ تـمـثّـل عـن بعدٍ طوائلَها   أثْنَى ثـنـا ماثلٍ مـن دون تقصير

٨ ومن أُتيح لـه فـوزُ المثول لدى   أعتابها فهو يـمـسـى جدّ مغضور

٩ تُرَى لحوز ملاك الملك من بَشَرٍ   وللكمال كـمـا شاءت من الحور

١٠ الـلّـهُ كـمّـلـهـا خَـلْـقـاً وجمّلها   خُـلْـقـاً فأبرزها فى أحسن الصور

١١ وٱختارها لـمـقـام لا يليق سوى   بـهـا يـنـزَّه عـن ندٍّ وتـنـظـيـر

١٢ حـاز النساء وقد جانَسْنَ فطرتها   أبْـهَـى سـنـاءٍ يباهى كلَّ مفطور

١٣ ما للمذكَّر بـعـد الآن مِـنْ شرفٍ   عـلـى المؤنَّث أو ذِكْـرٍ وتصدير

١٤ ذكـيّـةُ الأصل والأفعال مدحتُها   زكـوة كـلّ مقالٍ فرضُ تـكـفـيـر

١٥ لـو لـم تكن هذه الدنيا لنا وطناً   حلّتْ من الأوج مغنى غير منظور

١٦ ولـو تـخـلّـد إنسـانًـا مـحامـدُه   لكان تـخـلـيـدُها بدءَ الـتـقـاديـر

١٧ كأنّـمـا الـلّـه آتـاهـا مـآربَـهـا   على ٱقتراحٍ كـمـا تهوى وتخيير

١٨ طوبى لقطرٍ تجلَّتْ فـيـه حضرتُها   فـإنّـه مـتـحـلٍّ بـالـتـبـاشـيـر

١٩ إن تُحْجَب الشمس عنه فهو من خجلٍ   فـإنّ طـلـعـتـهـا أبْهَى مـن النور

---

13. Note the *jinās* and *ṭibāq*.
14. Note the *jinās*.
16. Note the *jinās*.
19. A typically Arab hyperbole on the English climate!

20 In *Her* days mankind live in comfort and affluence, and in Her exaltation do they exult above measure—

21 Through *Her* lustre the course of time is a constant festival, and all beings wear a shining aspect.

22 Security makes needless to them any guide to direct them, and peace secures them from dread of error or danger;

23 Fortune, who agitates and subverts other countries, and convulses them with commotion and change,

24 Causes no alteration whatever in *Her* kingdom, but remains there exempt from all disturbance;

25 While in the accomplishment of *Her* august designs the greatest and most formidable difficulties become small.

26 *She* attains the utmost of Her desires at a nod, whereas others would need a host to win the like success;

27 And whatever She purposes, Fortune seems to say to Her, "Be it as thou wilt! let prosperity and success attend thee!"

28 *She* has no need to repeat or be loud in Her commands, since Fortune is attentive to the smallest whisper of Her behest;

29 And, if duly portrayed, would be represented by a draughtsman as a slave with downcast eyes awaiting Her command.

30 None who take refuge within Her court will be oppressed or meet with any injury;

31 If the feeble approach Her door, Fortune endows them with the utmost strength.

32 Mankind are never unanimous except when they eulogize Her in prose or verse:

33 You may look the world through, but you will see none who do not praise Her.

34 If Her name is mentioned in a noble assembly, they are quite perfumed by its sweetness.

35 I wonder that my paper is not illumined by its brightness, or that my ink does not glitter through its beauty.

---

22. Note the *ṭibāq*.
24. Note the *jinās* and *ṭibāq*.
25. Note the *jinās* and *ṭibāq*.
28. Note the *ṭibāq*.

٢٠ تَنَعَّمَ الناس فى أيّامها رغدًا — ونُضِّروا بعلاها أىَّ تنضير

٢١ فالدهرُ أيّامُه عيدٌ ببهجتها — وطلعةُ الكون منها ذاتُ تنوير

٢٢ أغناهم الأمنُ عن هادٍ يدلّهمُ — والسلمُ عن حذر تضليلٍ وتغرير

٢٣ إن كدّر الدهرُ أصقاعًا ومال بها — وعاث فيها بإغراءٍ وتغيير

٢٤ فإنّه لم يحوّل فى ممالكها — حالاً ولكن صفا من كلّ تكدير

٢٥ خطيرةٌ صغّر الخطبُ الجليل لها — وكلُّ ذى خَطرٍ تصغيرَ تحقير

٢٦ تفوز بالأرب الأقصى إذا رمزت — ممّا يروم سواها بالجماهير

٢٧ إذا نَوَتْ خطّةً قال الزمانُ لها — لبّيك بشرى بتوفيقٍ وتيسير

٢٨ متى توجّس ركزًا من أوامرها — أغناه ذلك عن جهرٍ وتكرير

٢٩ فلو تصوّره شخصٌ تصوّره — فى زىّ عبدٍ غضيض الطرف مأمور

٣٠ ما ضِيمَ مستعصمٌ يومًا بعقوتها — ولا تخطّى إليه ضيرُ محذور

٣١ لو الدنىّ دنا من دون سدّتها — وافتْه دنياه بالأقصى من الزور

٣٢ تخالف الناسُ إلّا فى الثناء على — أخلاقها بين منظومٍ ومنثور

٣٣ ترى بعينَيْك هذا الكون أجمعه — وغير ذى المدح فيها غير منظور

٣٤ إذا ذكرتَ اسمها فى منتدى ملأٍ — تعطّروا من شذاه أىَّ تعطير

٣٥ عجبتُ للطرس لم ينضر برونقه — ولم يضئ حبرُه منه بتحبير

---

31. Note the *jinās*.
32. Note the *ṭibāq*.
34. Note the *jinās*.
35. Note the *jinās*.

36 If he who eulogizes Her is to blame for failing to extol Her sufficiently,

37 To be the known object of Her blame for one day is worth to him a whole life of honour:

38 But clemency is Her natural disposition, and one to be hailed as the noblest of all dispositions.

39 So numerous are the inventions of Her time, that Her approbation seems the inspirer of discovery;

40 *In the air* is the post of wires, that races with thought, and whispers every report:

41 *In the water* the sailing ships, on whose course Destiny attends,

42 That traverse the seas bearing the victorious flag to which every seaport is subject,

43 Wherein are kindled the fires of hospitality, and the fires of war, and those which subdue wind and storm:

44 *On the land* are the lines of iron in which may be recognised signs of industry and civilisation,

45 And many other things so admirable that none can praise them too much, or investigate them too thoroughly.

46 How excellent is that country, where truth is not depreciated, nor falsehood esteemed!

47 Go where you will, you will find what delights the eye, and what refreshes the mind, with nothing to displease.

48 Go to the right and there is security and prosperity, and go to the left and there is the facilitation of progress.

49 Its only fault is, that the eyes of men are perpetually dazzled by the splendour of its beauties,

50 And that there is no veil that conceals them from our eyes;

---

36. Note the *ṭibāq*.
37. Note the *jinās* and *ṭibāq*.
38. Note the *jinās*.
40. Perhaps the first reference in Arabic poetry to the telegraph. Note the *jinās*.
41. Koran, LV, 24 is quoted. Note the *jinās*.
43. The "fires of hospitality" of the British fleet must have become familiar to al-Shidyāq during his residence in Malta. The third fire mentioned in this astonishing couplet presumably was that lit in the stokehold of the ship.

٣٦ إن قصّر المدح عن أوصافها فغدا الـ   مطرى لِعَيٍّ ملوما غير معذور

٣٧ فإنّ تعزيرها يومًا لذى خطأٍ   إن صحّ ذلك عنها لهو تغرير

٣٨ لكنّما الحلم قد أضحى لها خُلُقًا   أَكْرِمْ بِخُلْقٍ على الإحسان مفطور

٣٩ كم من بدائع فى أيّامها ٱبتدعت   كأنّ مرضاتها وحىٌ لتدبير

٤٠ ففى الهواء بريد السلك ذا خطرٍ   مع الخواطر ينجو كلّ مأثور

٤١ وفى المياه الجوار المنشآت لها   مخر جرى معه جرىَ المقادير

٤٢ تطوى البحور وأعلامُ الفتوح بها   منشورة يتّقيها كلُّ ثغرور

٤٣ تُشَبُّ نارُ الوغى فيها ونارُ قرى   ونارُ تسخيرِ إعصارٍ وتيهور

٤٤ وإنّ وجه بسيط الأرض ذو سررٍ   من الحديد عليه فالُ تعمير

٤٥ وغير ذلك ممّا ليس يحصره   ترقين مُسْطِرٍ أوِ استئناف تنقير

٤٦ للّه درُّ بلادٍ لا يضيع بها   حقٌّ وما راج فيها قطّ من زور

٤٧ سِرْ أين شئتَ تجدْ للعين منتزهًا   والروح روحاً فلا مبذوء من بور

٤٨ ففى التيامن تأمين وميمنة   وفى التياسر تيسير لتسيير

٤٩ لا عيبَ فيها سوى أنّ النواظر من   شموسها فى حسورٍ غير محصور

٥٠ وأنّه لا دجى معْهنّ يستر من   عين الرقيب فما سرٌّ بمستور

---

44. An early reference to railways.
46. For the idiom, see Wright, II, 150A. Note the *ṭibāq*.
47. Note the *jinās*.
48. This ingenious line with its intricate pattern of complex *jinās* was not translated by its author.
49. Note the *jinās*.
50. Note the *jinās*.

51 And that its inhabitant is bewildered, having nothing to make him prefer one spot above another,

52 Since it is all equally pleasant and no choice can be made therein without perplexity.

53 Excellent island! that contains men who are like oceans of ever-flowing goodness.

54 No wonder that GOD has subjected the elements and the world to this noble people,

55 Because they are devoted to the good of mankind, to the improvement of countries, and the relief of their inhabitants.

56 How many benefits have they bestowed on others, that cannot be described by the pens of the most ingenious!

57 Benefits which are communicated by many Societies—one of them formed for the exercise of benevolence, another for the propagation of the Truth,

58 Another for the extension of knowledge and learning, another for the maintenance of peace among nations,

59 Another for the diffusion of charity, another for the preservation of reputation and honour,

60 Another for the liberation of slaves, another for the encouragement of liberality and kindness.

61 The changeableness of their weather does not change their disposition to do good.

62 They excel in sciences which were before unknown; and their object in practising them deserves the highest praise.

63 They have revived both philosophy and philanthropy, the former by books, the latter among men.

64 There remains not one place in the whole globe but the glory of the English nation is known in it.

65 If a traveller goes through a desert without a mark or sign, their fame will lead him as well as if there were any.

---

52. Note the *jinās*.
53. Note the *jinās* and implied *ṭibāq*.
54. Note the *jinās*.
55. Note the *jinās*.
57. Note the *jinās* and *ṭibāq*. An admirable catalogue of Victorian benevolent societies!

٥١ وأنّ محتلّها حيران ليس له … من اختيار لإحدى الساح والدور

٥٢ إذ كلّها مونقٌ بالحسن محتتنٌ … ما ريم تخييرها إلّا بتحيير

٥٣ نِعْمَ الجزيرة تحوى خيرَ من زخروا … بِرًّا بحور عطاءٍ غير مبتور

٥٤ لا غَرْوَ أن سخّر اللّه العناصر وال … دنيا لقومٍ كريمٍ أيَّ تسخير

٥٥ فإنّما دأبُهم نفع العباد وإِد … دابُ البلاد وإسعافُ المعاسير

٥٦ فكم لهم من يدٍ بيضاء تقصر من … بيانها الدهرَ أقلامُ النحارير

٥٧ فمِنْ قبيلٍ لبثّ الخير منتظمٍ … ومن قبيلٍ لنثّ الحقّ منثور

٥٨ ومن قبيلٍ لنشر العلم منتشرٍ … ومن قبيلٍ لعقد السلم مشهور

٥٩ ومن قبيلٍ ببذل المال مؤتجر … ومن قبيلٍ لصون العرض مأجور

٦٠ ومن قبيلٍ على عتق الرقيق وعرْ … ض العتق والطول والمعروف مقصور

٦١ ما أن يحيل حؤولٌ فى هوائهمُ … هوى نفوسهمُ عن مذهب الخير

٦٢ تبحّروا فى علومٍ لم تكن عُلِمَتْ … وحرّروا كلّ منطوق ومسفور

٦٣ للعلم والفضل نشرٌ منهمُ فلذا … بثٌّ وذاك خلود فى الأضابير

٦٤ لم يبق من مضربٍ فى الأرض ليس به … للإنكليز فخارٌ غير مذكور

٦٥ لو أنّ سفرًا تعنّى جوب مهمهةٍ … أغناه عن عَلَمٍ فيها وتؤمور

58. Note the *jinās*.
59. Note the *jinās*.
60. Note the *jinās*.
61. Note the double *jinās*.

66 What an honourable and generous people are they! whose goodness is acknowledged by all other nations.

67 Time would not suffice to enumerate the whole of their illustrious deeds, whether in writing or by word of mouth—

68 Deeds which they have achieved under the auspices of their noble Queen.

69 Not every one who bears a sceptre in his hand can reign with such authority, authority that cannot be excelled.

70 There may be a staff in the hands of one hero of Her army that will put down the highest sceptre.

71 Even the coward, if invested with Her authority, will become the conqueror of conquerors.

72 Ask Syria, when Her fleet appeared in its sea, what became of the castles of its former invaders;

73 Was not every man-of-war in it like an island walled by arms and ammunition?

74 And ask India, when some people thereof had shewn their ingratitude and revolted, how they were broken up.

75 And China, when she refused compliance, but boasted of her numerous population, was so humbled, that none could afterwards rise from their humiliation:

76 She was led to a point of submission which she had not at all contemplated.

77 And the Negroes, who in the most distant parts of the earth paid their homage, so that they were not exposed to any violence:

78 They were indeed savage, but they became happy, having been instructed in the arts of civilisation.

79 With them, when reduced into submission, the command of authority supplied the place of weapon.

80 This is true glory, not that which was related by the poets of ancient nations in former times.

81 Alexander the Great never attained to such power, nor could Caesar obtain it with his numberless host.

---

66. Note the *ṭibāq*.
72. Note the *jinās*.
74. Note the *ṭibāq*.

٦٦ أَنْعِمْ وأَكْرِمْ بقومٍ طاب محتدُهم   معروفهم فى البرايا غير منكور

٦٧ يفنى الزمان وما تحصى مآثرهم   سيّان فى كَلِمٍ يُرْوَى وتسطير

٦٨ سنّت لهم نيلهم أنفاسُ سيّدةٍ   مليكةٍ ذات تبجيلٍ وتوقير

٦٩ ما كلُّ من رُوِيَ الميحارُ فى يده   يحوز ملكاً كهذا غير مكثور

٧٠ فرُبَّ عودِ قناةٍ فى يدى بطلٍ   من جندها خافضٌ أَعْلَى المياحير

٧١ إذا تقلّد يوماً فى الوغى وَكَلْ   رضوانَها كان غلّاب المظافير

٧٢ سَلِ الشآم وقد عنّت بوارجُها   فى يمّها كيف أبراجُ المغاوير

٧٣ ألم تكن حين سارت كلُّ بارجةٍ   منها بضيعًا من الآلات ذا سور

٧٤ والهند إذ كفرت آلاءها فئةٌ   دانت وجمع وغاها جمع تكسير

٧٥ والصين لمّا أبتْ الّا منافرةً   ريضت فلم يك منها نفر نيفور

٧٦ قيدت إلى ضنك مضمار الخضوع ولم   يكن لها قبل عهدٌ بالمضامير

٧٧ والزنج بات بأَقْصَى الأرض ضارعةً   فما تصدَّتْ إلى أخذٍ بغشمير

٧٨ كانوا من الهمج الحمقى فأَسْعَدَهم   تمصيرُ ما بوّروه أيَّ تمصير

٧٩ أغناهمُ بعد أن حاق الوبالُ بهم   نشر المناشير عن نشر المناشير

٨٠ هذا هو الغرّ لا ما قيل من قِدَمٍ   عن القرون الخوالى فى الأساطير

٨١ ما حاز ذا الفخر ذو القرنين قطّ ولا   حواه قيصر بالقوم الحذافير

---

75. Note the *jinās*.
76. Note the *jinās*.
79. Note the quadruple *jinās*.

82 May God preserve Her kingdom from every revolution, and lead it on to power and victory!

83 The utmost desire of mankind is, that She should enjoy a long life, because the prolongation of Her life prolongs their happiness.

84 As also that Prince Albert and Her noble children should enjoy the same.

85 They are all as the sun, the moon, and the stars; but the sun in our language is feminine.

86 When the last of these stars appeared at the beginning of my task, I considered it to be a good omen.

87 If it is true as it is said, that the stars have an influence, then the best of it must be found in my words.

88 May God let the Queen of the age enjoy these real stars, her children, in health, and wealth, and godliness!

28 AL-BĀRŪDĪ

1 Was it the unsheathing of a sword, or the flicker of a lightning-flash, that illuminated for us about midnight the sky of Bāriq?

2 The riders bent their necks towards it in submission, with the sigh of one sorrowful and the glance of one moved by love;

3 And in the motions of the lightning is a sign of yearning, indicating what every lover seeks to conceal,

4 Unsealing eyelids to shed flowing tears, and slitting open breasts to disclose throbbing hearts.

5 And how should the secret of passion be comprehended by those not privy to passion, or how should the meaning of yearning be known to him who has never parted?

---

82. Note the *jinās*.
83. Note the *jinās*.
86. Arthur Duke of Connaught was born 1 May 1850.
87. Note the *jinās*.

28 Source: *Dīwān* (Cairo, 1948), II, 320–7.
Metre: *ṭawīl*.

٨٢ صان الاله مدى الازمان دولتها — عن كل دول بتأييد وتأزير

٨٣ قصار هذا الورى طول البقاء لها — فإنّ تعميرها ٱستبقاء تعمير

٨٤ وطول أعمار البرت الأمير وأو — لادٍ كرامٍ لها فخر الدهارير

٨٥ كالشمس والبدر والأنجام مطلعُهم — وعندنا الشمس أُنْثَى عُرْفَ تعبير

٨٦ لقد تفألتُ لمّا لاح آخرهم — عند ٱبتداء مديحى ذا بتبشير

٨٧ إن كان للنجم تأثيرٌ كما أثروا — ففى كلامىَ أضحى حسن تأثير

٨٨ ملّى المهيمن ما دام الزمان بهم — مليكة العصر فى عزٍّ وتظفير

٢٨ البارودى

١ أَسَلَّةُ سيفٍ أم عقيقةُ بارقِ — أضاءتْ لنا وهنًا سماوةَ بارقِ

٢ لوى الركبُ أعناقاً إليها خواضعاً — بزفرة محزونٍ ونظرةِ وامق

٣ وفى حركات البرق للشوق آيةٌ — تدلّ على ما جنّه كلُّ عاشق

٤ تفضّ جفوناً عن دموعٍ سوائلٍ — وتفرى صدوراً عن قلوبٍ خوافق

٥ وكيف يعى سرّ الهوى غيرُ أهله — ويعرف معنى الشوق من لم يفارق

This poem is one of the many fine odes composed by al-Bārūdī during his exile in Ceylon (1882–1900).

1. The conventional opening with the lightning-flash is cast in the form of a rhetorical question (*tajāhul al-ma'rūf*) and is decorated with a *jinās*. Bāriq is the name of several places, including one near Basra and others in Arabia, see Yāqūt, II, 32–3; here it is used metaphorically for Egypt.

3. The quivering of the lightning resembles the agitation of the lover's heart.

6 By passion's life (I swear), ever since sundering wasted me I have been in an annihilating distraction (derived) from the violence of emotion.

7 Sufficient exile has been my dwelling in Sarandīb, whereby I have stripped from me the garments of attachments.

8 Whoever desires to attain glory, let him show fortitude in confronting the fates and rushing blindly into difficult straits.

9 For if the days have muddied my drinking-place and blunted my edge by means of sudden calamities,

10 Yet no tribulation has changed me from my character, no trick (of destiny) has diverted me from my ways;

11 Rather I continue in the manner that delights me, and angers my enemies, and pleases my friends.

12 So my regret for being remote from a loyal friend is as my joy at being remote from an hypocritical enemy;

13 Then (balance) that with this—to escape from men is a precious prize, and the world is a snare of a cunning (huntsman).

14 Well now, you who find fault with me in your ignorance, not knowing that I am (as) a pearl upon the brows (of virtue),

15 Find consolation in meanness for missing sublimity, and go apart; the heights are not to be attained by using abusive language.

16 I am not one whose spirit accepts oppression, or who is content with what satisfies every fool;

17 If a man does not strive after what contains glory for him, he dies ignobly in the tents of young girls.

18 And what life is it for a man if, when circumstances change for the worse for him, he does not tie the thongs of his belt?

19 The summits of glory belong only to a man of nobility who, when he purposes, his resolve clears up every obscurity.

20 People say that I rebelled unrestrainedly; and those are habits that were never part of my character.

---

6. For the idiom see Wright, II, 79B, Lane 2155, col. I.

7. Sarandīb is the Arabic name for Ceylon. "The garments of attachments": the ties of country, family and friends.

10. Note the perfect *mulā'ama*.

٦ لَعَمْرُ الهوى إنّى لَدُنْ شفّنى النوى   لفى وَلَهٍ من سَوْرة الوجد ماحق

٧ كفى بمُقامى فى سَرَنْدِيبَ غُرْبَةً   نزعتُ بها عنّى ثيابَ العلائق

٨ ومن رام نَيْلَ العزّ فَلْيصطبرْ على   لقاءِ المنايا واْقتحامِ المضائق

٩ فإن تكن الأيّامُ رَنّقْنَ مشربى   وثلّمن حَدّى بالخطوب الطوارق

١٠ فما غيّرتنى محنةٌ عن خليقتى   ولا حوّلتنى خدعةٌ عن طرائقى

١١ ولكنّنى باقٍ على ما يَسُرُّنى   ويُغْضِبُ أعدائى ويُرْضِى أصادقى

١٢ فحسرةُ بُعْدى عن حبيبٍ مصادقٍ   كفرحة بُعْدى عن عدوٍّ مماذق

١٣ فتلك بهذى والنجاة غنيمةٌ   من الناس والدنيا مكيدةُ حاذق

١٤ ألا أيّها الزارى علىّ بجهله   ولم يَدْرِ أنّى دُرّةٌ فى المَفَارق

١٥ تَعَزَّ عن العلياء باللؤم واْعتزل   فإن العُلا ليست بلغو المناطق

١٦ فما أنا ممّن تقبل الضيمَ نفسُه   ويرضى بما يرضى به كلُّ مائق

١٧ إذا المرءُ لم ينهض لما فيه مجدُه   قضى وهْوَ كَلٌّ فى خدور العواتق

١٨ وأىُّ حياةٍ لامرئٍ إنْ تنكّرت   له الحالُ لم يعقد سيور المناطق

١٩ فما قُذُفاتُ العزِّ إلّا لماجدٍ   إذا همّ جلّى عزمُه كلَّ غاسق

٢٠ يقول أناسٌ إنّنى ثُرْتُ خالعًا   وتلك هناتٌ لم تكن من خلائقى

---

11. Note the *ṭibāq*.
12. Note the triple *ṭibāq*.
15. Note the *ṭibāq* and *jinās*.
20. The poet refers to the part which he played in the ʿArābī Pāshā rebellion.

21 Rather I proclaimed justice, seeking God's good pleasure, and I sought to arouse the people to defend their rights.

22 I bade to honour, and disapproved of dishonour, and that is a rule binding upon all God's creatures.

23 If the stand I took was disobedience, then I desired by my disobedience obedience to God.

24 Was the call for consultation a fault in me, seeing that in it is clear discrimination for those who desire right guidance?

25 Yes indeed, it is an obligation imposed by God upon every living being, alike the driven and the driver.

26 And how shall a man be free and refined, and yet be content with what every profligate performs?

27 If other people act hypocritically and with perfidy in religious matters, certainly I, praise be to God, am no hypocrite.

28 Moreover I have spared no pains in counselling a tribe whose treachery refused to accept the word of a truthful man.

29 They sought to govern the people by force, and hastened to destroy what the hands of compacts had constructed;

30 Then, when oppression continued, a party of soldiers stood up striving under the shadow of banners,

31 And there accompanied them the people of the country, and they advanced upon them swiftly, some coming and some joining,

32 Seeking of the lord of the land the execution of the sincere promises he had sworn to the people.

33 This then is the clear truth; so do not enquire of anyone but me, for I know well the facts.

34 O Egypt—may God lengthen your shadow, and may your soil be well watered with abundant sweet water from the Nile,

35 And may the hand of the zephyr not cease to bestow a sweet breath whose scent is healing to all who inhale it—

---

22. The frequent Koranic ordinance, see III, 100, 110, etc.

23. Note the *ṭibāq*.

24. The reference is to the proclamation of the Constitution by al-Bārūdī's 1882 Cabinet.

25. As set out in Koran, III, 153; XLII, 36.

27. Note the *jinās*.

٢١ ولكنّنى ناديتُ بالعدل طالباً — رضا اللّه واستنهضتُ أهل الحقائق

٢٢ أمرتُ بمعروفٍ وأنكرتُ منكَراً — وذلك حُكْمٌ فى رقاب الخلائق

٢٣ فإن كان عصيانًا قيامى فإنّنى — أردتُ بعصيانى إطاعةَ خالقى

٢٤ وهل دعوةُ الشورى علىّ غضاضةٌ — وفيها لمن يبغى الهدى كلُّ فارق

٢٥ بلى إنّها فرضٌ من اللّه واجبٌ — على كلّ حيٍّ من مسوقٍ وسائق

٢٦ وكيف يكون المرء حرّاً مهذّباً — ويرضى بما يأتى به كلُّ فاسق

٢٧ فإن نافق الأقوامُ فى الدين غدرةً — فإنّى بحمد اللّه غيرُ منافق

٢٨ على أنّنى لم آلُ نصحًا لمعشرٍ — أبى غدرُهم أن يقبلوا قولَ صادق

٢٩ رأوا أن يسوسوا الناسَ قهراً فأسرعوا — إلى نقض ما شادته أيدى الوثائق

٣٠ فلّما استمرّ الظلمُ قامت عصابة — من الجند تسعى تحت ظلّ الخوافق

٣١ وشايعهم أهل البلاد فأقبلوا — اليهم سراعًا بين آتٍ ولاحق

٣٢ يرومون من مولى البلاد نفاذ ما — تألّاه من وعدٍ إلى الناس صادق

٣٣ فهذا هو الحّق المبين فلا تَسَلْ — سواى فإنّى عالمٌ بالحقائق

٣٤ فيا مصر مدّ اللّه ظلّكِ وارتوى — ثراك بسلسالٍ من النيل دافق

٣٥ ولا برحت تمتار منك يدُ الصبا — أريجاً يداوى عَرْفُه كلّ ناشق

---

28. "A tribe": the Turco-Circassian officers controlling Egyptian affairs.
29. Note the *ṭibāq*.
30. The 'Arābī rebellion.
31. "The lord of the land": Khedive Tewfik.
33. Note the *jinās*.

36 You are the sanctuary of my people, the gathering-place of my family, the playground of my contemporaries, the arena of my predecessors,

37 A land where youth loosed my amulets, and hung upon my shoulders the harness of the Mashrafī sword.

38 When the Bihzād of my thought portrays her, she appears to my eyes in a charming guise of beauty.

39 I left there a noble family, and neighbours (the memory of) whose neighbourliness visits me every sunrise.

40 I forsook the sweetness of living after separation from them, and bade farewell to the comely prime of youth.

41 Now will the days grant me to meet them again, and will the yearner be happy with the object of his yearning in this world?

42 By my life, the period of separation has grown long, and broken to pieces are the cords that were formerly variously compacted.

43 Yet if the vicissitudes of the days prove evil, I am the first to trust in God's grace;

44 For sometimes affairs come straight again after they have been crooked, and maybe every expatriate returns to his fatherland.

29 SHAUQĪ

1 March has arrived; stand up with us, companion; greet the spring, the garden of the spirits,

2 And gather the boon-companions of the drinking-bowl under its banner, and spread in its courtyard the carpet of joy.

3 Serenity has been vouchsafed, so take for your soul its full share; serenity is not vouchsafed for a long period.

4 And sit in the laughing meadows, clapping in time to the antiphon of the strings and winecups,

---

37. "My amulets": the charms hung around a child's neck to avert the evil eye.

38. I have emended the reading *bahzārun* which is obviously wrong. Bihzād was the most famous of Persian miniature painters, who died *ca.* 1535; see *Encycl. of Isl.*², I, 1211.

41. Note the *jinās*.

42. Note the *ṭibāq*.

44. Note the double *ṭibāq*.

٣٦ فأنت حِمَى قومى ومشعب أسرتى ... وملعب أترابى ومَجْرَى سوابقى

٣٧ بلادٌ بها حلّ الشبابُ تمائمى ... وناط نِجادَ المشرفىّ بعاتقى

٣٨ إذا صاغها بِهْزادُ فكرى تصوّرت ... لعينَىَّ فى زىٍّ من الحسن رائق

٣٩ تركتُ بها أهلاً كراماً وجيرةً ... لهم جيرة تعتادنى كلّ شارق

٤٠ هجرتُ لذيذ العيش بعد فراقهم ... وودّعتُ ريعان الشباب الغُرانق

٤١ فهل تسمح الأيّامُ لى بلقائهم ... ويسعد فى الدنيا مشوقٌ بشائق

٤٢ لعمرى لقد طال النوى وتقطّعت ... وسائلُ كانت قبلُ شتّى المواثق

٤٣ فإن تكن الأيّامُ ساءت صروفُها ... فإنّى بفضل اللّه أوّلُ واثق

٤٤ فقد يستقيم الأمرُ بعد اعوجاجه ... ويرجع للأوطان كلُّ مفارق

٢٩ شوقى

١ آذارُ أقبلَ قُمْ بنا يا صاحِ ... حىِّ الربيع حديقة الأرواح

٢ واجمعْ نَدامَى الظرف تحت لوائه ... وانشرْ بساحته بساط الراح

٣ صفوٌ أُتيح فخذْ لنفسك قسطها ... فالصفو ليس على المدى بمُتاح

٤ واجلسْ بضاحكة الرياض مصفّقًا ... لتجاوُب الأوتار والأقداح

---

29 Source: *Dīwān* (Cairo, n.d.), II, 23–6.
Metre: *kāmil.*
This charming ode is dedicated to the English novelist Hall Caine, of the once popular romances.

1. For *ṣāḥi* (=*ṣāḥibu*) see Wright, II, 89A.

5 And seek the solace of a band of sakis radiant as stars, comely,

6 Their characters refined as the boon-companions of kings, embellished with virtue and forbearance.

7 And let your morning draught be a daughter of the two noble begetters—the vine, and the apple;

8 Whensoever you broach her barrel, and she laughs, the place is filled with radiance and sweet perfume.

9 Tyrannical she is, and when she remembers her noble origins she invests the inebriated with the robe of sobriety.

10 Pharaoh concealed her for the day of his triumphs, preparing her to be an offering to Ptah.

11 (Sit) between a minstrel whose bush is in the assemblies, and the veiled virgins of the bush in the great trees,

12 One warbling to his strings, whispering to one warbling loud on his branch—

13 White caps and black gowns, adorned with collars and anklets,

14 Chanting amidst their leaves melodies, like nuns on Easter morning

15 As they process between stalls and pulpits in a huge temple (hung) with brocade.

16 (March) the king of the plants—a whole earth is his abode, receiving him with marriage-feasts and rejoicings,

17 His banners of deep crimson and gleaming white spread amongst the hills.

18 The meadows have donned their embroideries for his coming, frolicking because of him in (every) nook and cranny.

19 Anon he covers the dwelling-places with narcissus' eyes, anon with the (gleaming) teeth of camomiles,

20 And heads of gilliflowers that have abased their crowns before his glory, redolent with perfume.

21 On the thrones of the twigs the open roses, facing one another, chant praises to him who is the opener,

---

10. Note the amusing *jinās*.

11. A *human* songbird contrasted with the actual songbirds in the garden.

٥ وٱستأنسنّ من السّقاة برُفقةٍ   غُرٍّ كأمثال النجوم صِباح
٦ رقّت كندمان الملوك خلالُهم   وتجمّلوا بمروءةٍ وسماح
٧ وٱجعلْ صَبوحَك فى البكور سليلةً   للمُنْجِبَيْنِ الكرم والتفّاح
٨ مهما فضضت دنانَها فٱستضحكت   مُلِئَ المكانُ سنىً وطيبَ نُفاح
٩ تَطْغَى فإن ذكرت كريمَ أصولها   خلعت على النشوان حلية صاحى
١٠ فرعونُ خبّأها ليوم فُتوحه   وأعدّ منها قربةً لفتاح
١١ ما بين شادٍ فى المجالس أيكه   ومحجَّباتِ الأيك فى الأدواح
١٢ غَردٍ على أوتاره يوحى إلى   غَردٍ على أغصانه صدّاح
١٣ بيضِ القلانس فى سواد جلاببٍ   حُلّينَ بالأطواق والأوضاح
١٤ رتّلنَ فى أوراقهنّ ملاحناً   كالراهبات صبيحة الإفصاح
١٥ يخطرنَ بين أرائكٍ ومنابرٍ   فى هيكلٍ من سندسٍ فيّاح
١٦ مَلِكُ النبات فكلُّ أرضٍ دارُه   تلقاه بالأعراس والأفراح
١٧ منشورةٌ أعلامُه من أحمرٍ   قانٍ وأبيضَ فى الربى لمّاح
١٨ لبست لمقدمه الخمائل وشيَها   ومرحْنَ فى كنفٍ له وجناح
١٩ يغشى المنازل من لواحظ نرجسٍ   آناً وآناً من ثغور أقاح
٢٠ ورؤوسِ منثورٍ خفضْنَ لعزّه   تيجانَهنّ عواطرَ الارواح
٢١ الوردُ فى سُرُر الغصون مفتّحٌ   متقابلٌ يُثنى على الفتّاح

---

13. A pretty description of the "veiled virgins of the bush".
21. Note the *jinās*.

22 Their sunlit cavalcades in the gardens distinguished from (other) blossoms by their thorns and weapons.

23 The morning breeze passes over the rose's cheeks, kissing (them), as the lips pass over the cheeks of beautiful maidens;

24 At night death strips off the beauty and radiance which the hand of dawn had woven for it.

25 The overthrow of the rose informs you—and all things pass away—that life is as a morning and an evening.

26 The snowy whites of the eglantine on their stems are like pearls mounted on the foreshafts of lances,

27 And the jasmine, delicate and pure, is as the secret thoughts of the gentle stroller,

28 Flashing through the twigs as if it were the effulgence of dawn in the daybreak of the branches.

29 And the pomegranate-blossom (has) blood upon its petals, crimson its letters like the seal of al-Saffāḥ.

30 The sorrowful violet is as a bereaved mother, meeting fate with fear and righteousness;

31 And over the pansies is a compassion and a grief like the thoughts of poets in (their) sorrows.

32 And the cypress in his ample robes displays his leg like a gay, pretty girl,

33 And the slender-statured palm-tree is turbaned and adorns itself with belts and sash

34 Like the daughters of Pharaoh watching processions under sunshades on a sunbaked day.

35 And you may behold (heaven's) plain like a wall of marble set in order with marvellous tablets,

36 The clouds therein like fat ostriches kneeling, and others circling on wing,

37 And the sun brighter than a bride, veiled on the day of the wedding-procession in a veil of shining gold,

---

28. The basic meaning of *bulja* is "clearness of the space between the eyebrows" (Lane 246, col. 1).

٢٢ ضاحى المواكب فى الرياض مميّزٌ　　دون الزهور بشوكةٍ وسلاح
٢٣ مرّ النسيمُ بصفحتَيْه مقبّلاً　　مرَّ الشفاه على خدود ملاح
٢٤ هتك الردى من حسنه وبهائه　　بالليل ما نسجتْ يدُ الإصباح
٢٥ ينبيك مصرعُه وكلٌّ زائلٌ　　أنّ الحياة كغدوةٍ ورواح
٢٦ ويقائقُ النسرين فى أغصانها　　كالدرّ رُكِّبَ فى صدور رماح
٢٧ والياسمينُ لطيفُه ونقيُّه　　كسريرة المتنزّه المِسْماح
٢٨ متألّقٌ خلَلَ الغصون كأنّه　　فى بُلجة الأفنان ضوءُ صباح
٢٩ والجلّنارُ دمٌ على أوراقه　　قانى الحروف كخاتم السفّاح
٣٠ وكأنّ محزون البنفسج ثاكلٌ　　يلقى القضاء بخشيةٍ وصلاح
٣١ وعلى الخواطر رقّةٌ وكآبةٌ　　كخواطر الشعراء فى الأتراح
٣٢ والسَّرْوُ فى الحِبَر السوابغ كاشفٌ　　عن ساقه كمليحةٍ مِفْراح
٣٣ والنخلُ ممشوقُ القدود معصَّبٌ　　متزيّنٌ بمناطق ووشاح
٣٤ كبنات فرعونٍ شهدن مواكبًا　　تحت المراوح فى نهارٍ ضاحِ
٣٥ وترى الفضاء كحائطٍ من مرمرٍ　　نُضِدَتْ عليه بدائعُ الألواح
٣٦ الغَيْمُ فيه كالنعام بدينةٌ　　بركتْ وأخرى حلّقت بجناح
٣٧ والشمس أبْهَى من عروسٍ بُرقعت　　يوم الزفاف بعسجدٍ وضّاح

---

29. Al-Saffāḥ (lit. "the blood-shedder") was the first of the Abbasid caliphs (reigned 750–4).

31. Note the *jinās* punning on "pensées".

38 And the water in the valley appears like conduits of quicksilver, or flung down sword-blades—

39 The sun of day has sent forth to it rays that are the ornaments of the swimming lotus,

40 The scatter of their shine on the leaves of the stalks like jewels flashing in the hollow of the palm.

41 And the water-wheels move like wailing-women in the villages, surprising the mourner with (their) sighing and lamentation—

42 The complainers who never knew true affection, the weeping women with (their) drenching tears.

43 Each (water-wheel) exposes its ribs, athirst, whilst the water (runs) through its bowels, (soon) parched (again),

44 Weeping when it is dilatory, laughing if it runs swiftly, like roan camels (divided) between sprightliness and fatigue.

45 The wheel is in chains and fetters, while its neighbour, blind, groans under his crushing yoke.

46 In spring and its beauty I recall the time of youth and its frolicsome young steed—

47 Was it aught but a flower like spring's blossoms, that annihilation hastened to overtake without any sin (committed)?

48 Hall Caine! Egypt is a story with which the hand of writers and commentators is never done.

49 Thereof (is a record) of papyrus, and Psalm, and Torah, and Koran, and Gospel,

50 And Menā, and Cambyses, and Alexander, and the two Caesars, and Ṣalāḥ (al-Dīn) the Great—

51 Those men and ages are a treasury; so stir your imagination, and it will bring the key.

52 The horizon of the land, with you (dwelling) in its quarters, is adorned with stars and lamps.

---

43. A clever description of the "weeping" water-wheels.
45. "Its neighbour" is of course the buffalo or camel harnessed to the wheel.

٣٨ الماءُ بالوادى يُخال مسارباً   من زئبقٍ أو مُلْقَيات صفاح

٣٩ بعثت له شمسُ النهار أشعّةً   كانت حُلَى النيلوفر السبّاح

٤٠ يزهو على ورق الغصون نثيرُها   زَهْوَ الجواهر فى بطون الراح

٤١ وجرت سواقٍ كالنوادب بالقُرَى   رُعْنَ الشجىَّ بأنّةٍ ونواح

٤٢ الشاكياتُ وما عرفن صبابةً   الباكياتُ بمدمعٍ سحّاح

٤٣ من كلّ بادية الضلوع غليلةٍ   والماءُ فى أحشائها مِلْواح

٤٤ تبكى إذا ونيتْ وتضحك إن هفتْ   كالعيس بين تنشُّطٍ ورزاح

٤٥ هى فى السلاسل والغلول وجارُها   أَعْمَى ينوء بنيره الفدّاح

٤٦ إنّى لأذكر بالربيع وحسنه   عهد الشباب وطِرفه المِمْراح

٤٧ هل كان إلّا زهرةً كزهوره   عجل الفناءُ لها بغير جُناح

٤٨ هول كين مصرُ روايةٌ لا تنتهى   منها يدُ الكتّاب والشُّرّاح

٤٩ فيها من البُرْدىّ والمزمور وال   توراة والفرقان والإصحاح

٥٠ ومِنَا وقمبيزٍ الى إسكندرٍ   فالقيصرَيْن فذى الجلال صلاح

٥١ تلك الخلائق والدهور خزانةٌ   فابعثْ خيالك يأت بالمفتاح

٥٢ أفق البلاد وأنت بين ربوعها   بالنجم مزدانٌ وبالمصباح

---

52. "Lamps": *miṣbāḥ* can mean "asterism"; see Lane 1643, col. 2.

30 MAṬRĀN

1 He raised up and raised high, and built and reinforced, not for the sake of grandeur, not even for himself, but for the grave,

2 Enslaving his nation in his own day, enslaving his sons to the aggressor tomorrow.

3 I behold here numerous as the sands creatures too many to be numbered,

4 Pale of face and wet of brow, like dry herbage sprinkled over with dew,

5 Their backs bent, their footsteps silent, like ants crawling along lowly, unceasing,

6 Gathered together like seas, branching off like rivers, descending, ascending.

7 Are all these souls, perishing tomorrow, building for one due to perish an eternal tomb?

8 You dead ones! are you not made to hear by the voice of the herald, declaring and repeating?

9 Rise up, and behold the common herd around you trampling the heads of kings now blackened with age.

10 Rise up, and behold the aggressor in your lands, ruling over them tyrannical and mighty.

11 Rise up, and behold your bodies exposed in an exhibition to all who seek a spectacle—

12 A resurrection (indeed), when you are taken to account for your actions by every one of us who passes.

13 It did not avail you, that the building was lofty, the land despoiled, the kings reduced to slaves;

14 Yet fair fame would have availed you, had you built the tomb low, and raised up with right guidance.

15 He errs, who imagines that the grave is a magic charm for him, protecting him by death from death!

---

30 Source: Khalīl Maṭrān, *al-Ṭughāt* (ed. Ra'ūf Khūrī, Beirut, 1949), 12–13.
Metre: *rajaz*.
A Lebanese view of the Pyramids.

1. Note the *jinās*.
2. Note the *mulā'ama*.
3. Note the *jinās*.
4. Note the *jinās*.
6. Note the double *ṭibāq* and partial *jinās*.

٣٠ مطران

١ شاد فأعْلَى وبنى فوطّدا   لا للعُلَى ولا له بل للعِدَى

٢ مستعبِدٌ أمّتَه فى يومه   مستعبَدٌ بنيه للعادى غدا

٣ إنّى أرى عَدَّ الرمال ههنا   خلائقاً تكثر أن تُعَدَّدا

٤ صُفْرَ الوجوه نادياً جِباهُهم   كالكلأ اليابس يعلوه الندى

٥ محنيّةً ظهورُهم خُرْسَ الخُطَى   كالنمل دبَّ مستكيناً مخْلِدا

٦ مجتمعين أبْحُرًا منفرعيـ   ن أنْهُرًا منحدرين صُعَّدا

٧ أكُلُّ هذى الأنفس الهلكى غدًا   تبنى لفانٍ جَدَثًا مخلَّدا

٨ يا أيّها الموتى ألَمْ يُسْمِعْكُمُ   صوتُ المنادى صادعًا مردِّدا

٩ قوموا ٱنظروا السوقة فيما حولكم   تدوس هاماتِ الملوك هُمَّدا

١٠ قوموا ٱنظروا العادِيَ فى أمصاركم   يحكم فيها مستبدًّا أيِّدا

١١ قوموا ٱنظروا أجسادكم معروضةً   فى مشهدٍ لمن يروم المشهدا

١٢ بَعْثٌ به يسألكم حسابَ ما   قدّمتُمُ مَنْ راحَ منّا وٱغتدى

١٣ لم يُغْنِكم منه البناء عالياً   والأرضُ نهباً والملوكُ أعْبُدا

١٤ وكان يُغْنِيكم جميلُ الذكر لو   خفضتم اللحد وشِدْتم بالهدى

١٥ أخطأ مَن توهَّم القبر له   حرزاً يقيه بالردى من الردى

---

7. Note the *ṭibāq*.
8. "The herald": as on the Day of Resurrection, see Koran, L, 40.
9. Note the *ṭibāq*.
10. "The aggressor": the British.
11. "An exhibition": in the museums.
12. "Every one of us who passes": lit. "those of us who go in the evening and those who go in the morning".
13. Note the *ṭibāq* and triple *tamyīz*.

31 AL-RUṢĀFĪ

1 Comrade, affairs are in a ferment; what calamities will night and day bring (upon us)?

2 Glory be to the Lord of men! Every day He is engaged in some almighty enterprise;

3 The Creator of being, the Glorious, is Pre-Eternal, One—in His sight the centuries are (as but) seconds.

4 All that His Kingdom enfolds is Words (by Him spoken), and to Him finally reverts every Meaning.

5 We have today a bubbling of events like the bubbling of cooking-pots on stoves.

6 Surely I perceive the harbingers of a dawn diffusing itself over the shadows of desires;

7 That blood (shed) in the war is merely a twilight of its crimson radiance.

8 Surely I descry a revolution of the changes of time embracing every place,

9 Whereby the near will appear far, and the far will appear near,

10 And the revered will be other than revered, and the despised will be other than despised,

11 And the weak will become respected as to his right, and the tyrant will end in utter loss.

12 The Pleiades will mount up in security from the aggression of Capella and Aldebaran,

13 And the Milky Way will show forth as a she-camel cleaving to her young, the twin stars of Ursa Minor drawing near to her Taurus.

14 The Lord of the heavens and earth will reveal Himself to us in His justice and compassion,

---

31 Source: *Dīwān* (Cairo, 1373/1953), 476–7.
Metre: *khafīf*.

1. For *yuṭarriqu*, see Lane 1846.
2. A reference to Koran, LV, 29.
3. For the abbreviated form *thawānī*, see Wright, II, 388 c.
4. An echo of Koran, VI, 115; XVIII, 109.

٣١ الرصافى

١ صاحِ إنّ الخطوب فى غليانٍ   فبماذا يُطَرِّقُ المَلَوانِ

٢ جلّ ربُّ الأنام فى كلّ يومٍ   هو من كبريائه فى شأن

٣ خالِقُ الكون ذو الجلال قديمٌ   واحدٌ عنده القرون ثوانى

٤ كلّ ما ضمّ ملكهُ كلماتٌ   وإليه ٱنتهتْ جميع المعانى

٥ نسمع اليوم للخطوب أزيزًا   كأزيز القدور فى الفوران

٦ إنّنى مبصرٌ تباشير صبحٍ   مستفيضٍ على ظلام الأمانى

٧ ليس تلك الدماء فى الحرب إلّا   شفقاً من ضيائه الأرجوانى

٨ إنّنى أستشفّ من غِيَر الدهـ   ـر انقلابًا يعمّ كلّ مكان

٩ سيلوح الدانى به وهْو قاصٍ   ويلوح القاصى به وهو دان

١٠ ويكون المُعَزّ غير مُعَزٍّ   ويكون المُهان غير مُهان

١١ وسيغدو الضعيف محترمَ الحـ   ـقّ ويمسى الظلوم فى خسران

١٢ والثريّا ستعتلى فى أمانٍ   من عداء العيّوق والدبران

١٣ وستبدو أمّ النجوم رؤوساً   يتدانى من ثورها الفرقدان

١٤ يتجلّى ربّ السماوات والأر   ض علينا بعدله والحنان

---

6. Note the *ṭibāq*.
9. Note the *ṭibāq* and *mulā'ama*.
10. Note the *ṭibāq* and *mulā'ama*.
11. Note the double *ṭibāq*.
12. For the astronomical images, cf. the aubade by Ibn Hāni' translated in my *Moorish Poetry*, 84–8.

15 And the colonialists will acknowledge defeat, and the lands will shine forth in prosperity.

16 Company of Arabs! Where will you stand amongst the people, when Time's revolution is complete?

17 Asleep, whilst Destiny opens amongst you the two eyes of a waker, its day and night?

18 The people have broken compact with you before this, and have made light of keeping it in the taverns;

19 They have held in contempt their promise and gone back on it, and they have exploited the buried treasures of the homelands,

20 And they have established there air bases to muster armies and aircraft.

21 Then they disseminated spies therein, working mischief and corruption in its courtyards and edifices.

22 Then they proceeded to rule the country like a ship in which they held the rudder.

23 All this, whilst you are independent—so they allege—by grace of themselves.

24 They have fettered you with treaties for their benefit, (treaties) speaking ostensibly of your interest;

25 Thereby they have fastened you firmly in bondage, and said, "This is nothing but a kindness to you".

26 Those treaties, O people, are simply like treaties of wolves with lambs.

27 Do you not remember how your ancestors were scornful when they were treated with misprision?

28 The day when they rode out, glory accompanying their ranks, (armed) with the ridged Indian sword,

29 And their banners fluttered on high, in armies to which East and West submitted.

30 So arise today, seeking to renew a glory such as that which surpassed the sun and the moon.

---

15. Note the *jinās*. The "colonialists" were of course the British.
16. Note the *ṭibāq*.
18. "The people": the British.

١٥	فيبوءِ المستعمرون بخسرٍ	وتضىء البلادُ بالعمران
١٦	معشرَ العُرب أين أنتم من القو	م إذا ما تمّ انقلاب الزمان
١٧	أنيامٌ والدهر يفتح فيكم	من جديدَيْه مقلتَى يقظان
١٨	نقض القوم عهدكم قبل هذا	واستخفّوا بحفظه فى الحوانى
١٩	واستهانوا بالوعد إذ أخلفوه	واستغلّوا دفائن الاوطان
٢٠	وأقاموا بها قواعد جوٍّ	لاحتشاد الجنود والطيران
٢١	ثم بثّوا بها العيون يعيثو	ن فسادًا فى سوحها والمبانى
٢٢	ثم ساروا بحكمها سَيْر فُلْكٍ	هم بها آخذون بالسُكّان
٢٣	كلّ هذا وأنتم مستقلّو	ن بزعمٍ من عندهم وٱمتنان
٢٤	قيّدوكم لنفعهم بعهودٍ	ناطقاتٍ من أمركم بلسان
٢٥	أوثقوكم بها إسارًا وقالوا	ليس هذا لكم سوى إحسان
٢٦	ليس تلك العهود يا قوم إلاّ	كعهود الذئاب للحُمْلان
٢٧	أفلا تذكرون فى أوّليكم	أَنَفًا من مسيسهم بهوان
٢٨	يوم ساروا والعزّ فيهم يماشى	حزبهم بالمشطّب الهندوانى
٢٩	وتعالت راياتهم خافقاتٍ	فى جيوشٍ عنا لها الخافقان
٣٠	فٱنهضوا اليوم مستجدّين مجدًا	كالذى كان دونه القمران

19. "Buried treasures": presumably the oil-fields.
20. A reference in particular to the former R.A.F. base at Habbaniya.
29. Note the *jinās*.

31 Glory has a lofty place in earnest strivings, not to be attained by the laggard.

32 Tell him who seeks to split and divide us, "You are like a goat butting against rocks!

33 Out upon you! Islam has united us in a unity like the unity of the All-Merciful,

34 And we have laid hold of it by a firm cord, the cord of brotherhood and faith."

35 The meaning of our unitarian belief in God, our religion, is none other than our unification as an entity.

36 For this, yea, for this, for this we believe in the Unity of the Supreme Judge—

37 A unity not impaired by the successive vicissitudes of ages and times,

38 A unity regarding which there came to us from God a Messenger with the Book and the Discrimination,

39 (A unity) whereby a God Pre-Eternal, One, has guided us, in Whose sight the centuries are (as but) seconds.

40 We do not consider that any creature has authority over us, only the authority of the Creator of beings.

---

33. Note the *jinās*.
34. See Koran, III, 98, 108.
35. The poet refers to the Arab Unity movement. Note the *jinās*.

٣١ إنّ للمجد فى المساعى محلًّا   عاليًا لا يحلّه المتوانى

٣٢ قُلْ لمن رام صدْعنا بشقاقٍ   أنت كالوعل ناطح الصفْوان

٣٣ وَيْكَ إنّ الإسلام أوحد فينا   وحدةً مثل وحدة الرحمن

٣٤ فاْعتصمنا منها بحبلٍ وثيقٍ   هو حبل الإخاء والإيمان

٣٥ ليس معنى توحيدنا الله فى الملّـ   ـة إلاّ اْتّحادنا فى الكيان

٣٦ فلهذا نَعَمْ لهذا لهذا   نحن دِنّا بوحدة الديّان

٣٧ وحدة لا يفلّها المتوالى   من صروف الدهور والأزمان

٣٨ وحدة جاءنا من الله فيها   مُرْسَلٌ بالكتاب والفرقان

٣٩ فهدانا بها إلهٌ قديمٌ   واحدٌ عنده القرون ثوانى

٤٠ ما نرى سلطةً علينا لخلقٍ   غير سلطان خالق الأكوان

---

36. Note the *jinās*.
40. Note the *jinās*.

BIOGRAPHICAL NOTES

Abbreviations

Abd-el-Jalil = J.-M. Abd-el-Jalil, *Brève Histoire de la Littérature Arabe.* Paris, 1947.

EI[1] = *Encyclopaedia of Islam.*

EI[2] = *Encyclopaedia of Islam.* New Edition. (In progress.)

GAL = C. Brockelmann, *Geschichte der arabischen Litteratur*, with Supplements.

Gibb = H. A. R. Gibb, *Arabic Literature.* 2nd edition. Oxford, 1963.

Lyall = C. J. Lyall, *Ancient Arabian Poetry.* London, 1930.

Nicholson = R. A. Nicholson, *A Literary History of the Arabs.* London, 1907.

Nykl = A. R. Nykl, *Hispano-Arabic Poetry.* Baltimore, 1946.

AL-SAMAU'AL ibn Gharīḍ ibn 'Ādiyā' flourished in the middle of the sixth century A.D. Said to be a member of a Jewish Arab tribe, he dwelt in the fortress of al-Ablaq near Taimā' where he is reported to have sheltered the poet Imra' al-Qais fleeing before King al-Mundhir of al-Ḥīra. His name was proverbial for fidelity.

EI[1], IV, 133; *GAL*, I, 28–9, Suppl. I, 59–60; Nicholson, 84–5; Abd-el-Jalil, 44.

AL-NĀBIGHA, Ziyād ibn Mu'āwiya, of the Banū Dhubyān, who died *ca.* A.D. 604, was attached to the court of the Lakhmids of al-Ḥīra and became their chief panegyrist, before being constrained to flee for his life to the Ghassānids whose hospitality he praised with equal eloquence.

EI[1], III, 804–5; *GAL*, I, 22, Suppl. I, 45; Nicholson, 121–3; Lyall, 95–102; Gibb, 22, 26; Abd-el-Jalil, 41.

'ANTARA ibn Shaddād, the "Black Knight" of the Banū 'Abs, son of an Arab father and an Abyssinian mother, one of the greatest hero-poets of the sixth century and author of a *Mu'allaqa* (see my *Seven Odes*, 148–84), became in medieval Islam the central figure of an extensive popular romance.

EI[2], I, 521; *GAL*, I, 22, Suppl. I, 45; Nicholson, 114–16; Gibb, 23, 27; Abd-el-Jalil, 38–9.

AL-KHANSĀ', Tumāḍir bint 'Amr ibn al-Sharīd, of the Banū Sulaim, the greatest of Arab poetesses, born towards the end of the sixth century, is chiefly renowned for the poignant elegies which she composed on the slaying of her brothers Mu'āwiya and Ṣakhr.

EI[1], II, 901–2; *GAL*, I, 40, Suppl. I, 70; Nicholson, 126–7; Gibb, 18; Abd-el-Jalil, 45.

'UMAR IBN ABĪ RABĪ'A (*ca.* 23–101/643–719) of the Banū Quraish, son of a wealthy merchant of Mecca, employed his abundant leisure and great talents in pursuing and celebrating the charms of beautiful women, so that his verses came to be called "the greatest crime ever committed against God". To him belongs in large measure the credit for detaching the *nasīb* (amatory prelude) from the *qaṣīda* and for polishing the language of love-poetry into an almost conversational ease.

EI[1], III, 979; *GAL*, I, 45–7, Suppl. I, 76–7; Nicholson, 237; Gibb, 44; Abd-el-Jalil, 69–70.

BASHSHĀR IBN BURD (*ca.* 95–167/714–83), son of a Persian freedman of Basra and blind from birth, rose to fame in Umayyad and Abbasid court-circles as a poet of brilliant encomia, mordant satire and scandalous licence. His compositions (many ascribed to him are of very doubtful authenticity) mark the beginnings of the *badī'* style.

EI[2], I, 1080–2; *GAL*, I, 73–4, Suppl. I, 108–10; Nicholson, 373–4; Gibb, 61; Abd-el-Jalil, 95.

ABŪ NUWĀS, al-Ḥasan ibn Hāni' al-Ḥakamī (*ca.* 130–98/747–813), son of an Arab father and a Persian mother, was born in Ahwaz, educated in Basra and Kufa, then moved to Baghdad where he rapidly established himself as the poet-laureate of love and wine. Enjoying the protection of the Barmecides, he had to flee to Egypt on their fall but returned to close favour with the caliph al-Amīn. He led the reaction against the old desert conventions of poetry; his style is simple and melodious.

EI[2], I, 143–4; *GAL*, I, 74–6, Suppl. I, 114–18; Nicholson, 292–6; Gibb, 62–3; Abd-el-Jalil, 95–8.

ABU 'L-'ATĀHIYA, Ismā'īl ibn al-Qāsim (130–210/748–825), of Kufa and later of Baghdad, in his youth wrote much in praise of women and wine but later repented and specialised in preaching the virtues of the godly life and the emptiness of worldly power and pleasures.

EI[2], I, 108–9; *GAL*, I, 77–8, Suppl. I, 119–20; Nicholson, 296–303; Gibb, 63; Abd-el-Jalil, 98–9.

ABŪ TAMMĀM, Ḥabīb ibn Aus al-Ṭā'ī (*ca.* 190–230/805–45), son of a Christian wine-merchant of Damascus, studied in Cairo and panegyrised the governor of Syria and later the caliphs and leading personalities of Baghdad. In addition to his own admired compositions (though their merits have been much discussed in both antiquity and modern times) he also published a famous anthology of ancient poems.

*EI*², I, 153–5; *GAL*, I, 83–5, Suppl. I, 134–7; Nicholson, 129–30; Gibb, 85; Abd-el-Jalil, 100–1.

IBN AL-RŪMĪ, 'Alī ibn al-'Abbās (221–83/836–96), apparently of Byzantine descent (on which account some modern Arab critics have found Greek elements in his style), was born in Baghdad where he passed most of his life as panegyrist and lampoonist. His descriptive verse is highly appreciated.

*EI*¹, II, 410; *GAL*, I, 79, Suppl. I, 123–5; Gibb, 85; Abd-el-Jalil, 102.

AL-BUḤTURĪ, Abū 'Ubāda al-Walīd ibn 'Ubaid Allāh (206–84/821–97), born at Manbij in Syria and befriended by Abū Tammām, practised the art of panegyric in his native province and in Baghdad, where he intermittently enjoyed the favour of successive caliphs. Like Abū Tammām he also collected ancient poems.

*EI*², I, 1289–90; *GAL*, I, 80, Suppl. I, 125–7; Nicholson, 324; Gibb, 85; Abd-el-Jalil, 101–2.

IBN AL-MU'TAZZ, Abu 'l-'Abbās 'Abd Allāh (247–96/861–908), son of the caliph al-Mu'tazz by a slave mother, spent most of his life remote from politics in literary and learned circles, but on the death of the caliph al-Muktafī was persuaded to accept the throne, an honour he enjoyed for but a day, being then assassinated. Apart from his poetry he also wrote important books on poetics and related topics.

*EI*¹, II, 406; *GAL*, I, 80–1, Suppl. 128–30; Nicholson, 325; Gibb, 86; Abd-el-Jalil, 99–100.

AL-MUTANABBĪ, Abu 'l-Ṭaiyib Aḥmad ibn al-Ḥusain al-Ju'fī (303–54/915–65), born of a humble Kufan family, studied at Damascus and in the Bedouin tents. After a term of imprisonment for imposture (his name means "the Would-be Prophet"), his great poetic gifts commended him to the Ḥamdānid Saif al-Daula who rewarded him munificently for his encomia. Falling out with his powerful patron, he fled to Egypt but was disappointed by Kāfūr the negro ex-slave Ikhshīdid. On his way to the Buwaihid court in Shiraz he was murdered by brigands. He is accounted the most sublime of the classical poets, and many of his phrases have become proverbs.

*EI*¹, III, 781–4; *GAL*, I, 86–8, Suppl. I, 138–42; Nicholson, 304–13; Gibb, 91–2; Abd-el-Jalil, 157–9.

ABŪ FIRĀS, al-Ḥārith ibn Sa'īd ibn Ḥamdān al-Ḥamdānī (320–57/932–68), whose mother was a Byzantine, was first cousin of Saif al-Daula.

He was captured during the wars against Byzantium, and his "prison-poems" of complaint and entreaty are greatly admired.

EI[2], I, 119–20; *GAL*, I, 88, Suppl. I, 142–4; Nicholson, 304; Gibb, 90.

AL-SHARĪF AL-RAḌĪ, Abu 'l-Ḥasan Muḥammad ibn al-Ḥusain (359–406/970–1015), a direct descendant of the caliph 'Alī and a leading Shī'ite, was born in Baghdad and promoted by the Buwaihid Bahā' al-Daula. In addition to composing a large number of poems, many of an anti-Sunnī turn, he also wrote two treatises on the Koran.

EI[1], IV, 329–30; *GAL*, I, 82, Suppl. I, 131–2; Gibb, 98.

MIHYĀR AL-DAILAMĪ, Abu 'l-Ḥasan ibn Marzūya (d. 428/1037), was converted from Zoroastrianism to Islam by al-Sharīf al-Raḍī, thereafter residing in Baghdad and preaching Shī'ism.

GAL, I, 82, Suppl. I, 132.

AL-MA'ARRĪ, Abu 'l-'Alā' Aḥmad ibn 'Abd Allāh (363–449/973–1058), born in northern Syria and blinded in early childhood, studied under the grammarian Ibn Khālawaih and other famous scholars and soon displayed a gift for poetry. After wide travels which did not always please him, he returned home and expressed his free-thinking and pessimistic philosophy in famous prose and verse, notably the *Risālat al-Ghufrān* and the *Luzūmīyāt*.

EI[1], I, 75–7; *GAL*, I, 254–5, Suppl. I, 449–54; Nicholson, 313–24; Gibb, 92–4; Abd-el-Jalil, 159–62.

IBN ZAIDŪN, Abu 'l-Walīd Aḥmad ibn 'Abd Allāh (394–463/1003–71), born in Cordova, was involved in Andalusian politics and spent some time in prison. Famous for his unsuccessful courtship of the poetess Wallāda, he was a fine prose-writer as well as amongst the greatest poets of Moorish Spain.

EI[1], II, 429–30; *GAL*, I, 274–5, Suppl. I, 485; Nicholson, 424–6; Gibb, 112–13; Nykl, 106–20; Abd-el-Jalil, 195.

IBN AL-KHAIYĀṬ, Shihāb al-Dīn Aḥmad ibn Muḥammad (458–517/1066–1123) was born in Damascus and travelled extensively, visiting Persia amongst other lands, returning to die in his native city.

GAL, I, 253, Suppl. I, 448.

IBN KHAFĀJA, Abū Isḥāq Ibrāhīm ibn Abi 'l-Fatḥ (450–533/1058–1138), born near Valencia, lived privately in his native town of Alcira where he died, leaving a large collection of poems.

GAL, I, 272, Suppl. I, 480–1; Nykl, 227–31.

IBN ZUHR, Abū Bakr Muḥammad ibn 'Abd al-Malik (504–96/1110–1200), born in Seville, was a member of a famous learned family and became a distinguished physician, enjoying the patronage in Marrakesh of the Almohed Ya'qūb ibn Yūsuf al-Manṣūr.

EI[1], II, 431; *GAL*, I, 489, Suppl. I, 893; Gibb, 111; Nykl, 248–51.

IBN 'UNAIN, Sharaf al-Dīn Muḥammad ibn Naṣr Allāh (549–630/1154–1233), born in Damascus, satirised Ṣalāḥ al-Dīn (Saladin) and so went into exile, travelling as far afield as India and Yemen. After the death of Ṣalāḥ al-Dīn he returned to Damascus where he enjoyed the patronage of the ruler and was promoted vizier.

GAL, I, 318, Suppl. I, 551.

IBN AL-FĀRIḌ, Sharaf al-Dīn Abu 'l-Qāsim 'Umar ibn 'Alī (577–632/1182–1235), son of a Cairo notary, lived the life of a Sufi and is buried at the foot of the Mokattam hills.

EI[1], III, 980; *GAL*, I, 262, Suppl. I, 462–5; Nicholson, 394–8; Abd-el-Jalil, 162–3.

BAHĀ AL-DĪN ZUHAIR ibn Muḥammad al-Muhallabī (581–656/1186–1258), born in Mecca, migrated young to Egypt and there entered the service of the Aiyūbid Sultans. Later he fell from grace and went into exile. His last days in Cairo were spent in poverty.

EI[2], I, 912–13; *GAL*, I, 264, Suppl. I, 465; Gibb, 130–1.

IBN SAHL, Abū Isḥāq Ibrāhīm al-Isrā'īlī (d. 658/1260), a Jew of Seville who accepted conversion to Islam, left behind a small but exquisite collection of mannered lyrics.

GAL, I, 273–4, Suppl. I, 485; Nykl, 344–5.

IBN ZĀKŪR, Abū 'Abd Allāh Muḥammad ibn Qāsim al-Fāsī (d. 1120/1708), born at Fez and educated in Marrakesh, Tetuan and Algiers, was a learned scholar as well as a poet, composing over a dozen treatises.

GAL, Suppl. II, 684.

AL-SHIDYĀQ, (Aḥmad) Fāris ibn Yūsuf (1801–87), born in the Lebanon of a Maronite Christian family, migrated first to Cairo, then lived in Malta, England, France, Tunis (where he became a Muslim) and finally Turkey. He edited the influential *al-Jawā'ib* and played a prominent part in Muslim politics.

GAL, II, 505, Suppl. II, 867–8; Abd-el-Jalil, 224.

AL-BĀRŪDĪ, Maḥmūd Sāmī (1839–1904), Egyptian statesman, exiled in Ceylon from 1883 to 1900, played a leading part in the renaissance of Arabic literature.

EI[2], I, 1069–70; *GAL*, Suppl. III, 7–18; Abd-el-Jalil, 239.

SHAUQĪ, Aḥmad (1868–1932), born in Cairo, was poet-laureate to the Khedivial House; from 1914 to 1919 he lived in exile in Spain. He pioneered the poetical drama in Arabic, and composed many fine odes and lyrics in a variety of styles.

GAL, Suppl. III, 21–48; Abd-el-Jalil, 239–40.

MAṬRĀN, Khalīl (1870–1949), born in the Lebanon and a pupil of Ibrāhīm al-Yāzijī, migrated to Cairo where he became a prominent journalist, but later dedicated himself to poetry; he also translated Shakespeare's *Othello* and *Merchant of Venice*.

GAL, Suppl. III, 86–96; Abd-el-Jalil, 241.

AL-RUṢĀFĪ, Ma'rūf (1875–1945), born in Baghdad of Kurdish parents, taught in Istanbul and Jerusalem and then entered politics, serving for a time as Iraqi Minister of Education. He was a spokesman of Arab Unity.

GAL, Suppl. III, 488–9; Abd-el-Jalil, 242.

18670036R00109

Printed in Great Britain
by Amazon